**DIESTERWEGS NEUSPRACHLICHE BIBLIOTHEK**

*Arbeitsbuch Basisfach*

# The Ambiguity of Belonging

**Erarbeitet von**
Christoph Deeg
Katja Krey
Florian Nuxoll
Gerburg Rolvering

*Diesterweg*
*westermann*

## Unsere Materialien für das Basisfach Englisch:

**The Ambiguity of Belonging**
Arbeitsbuch Basisfach
11,95 € ❑ / 120 Seiten
ISBN: 978-3-425-04997-9

**Gran Torino**
DVD
9,95 € ▼
ISBN: 978-3-425-04995-3

**The Ambiguity of Belonging**
Lehrerhandreichung Basisfach
10,00 € ◆ / 100 Seiten
ISBN: 978-3-425-04989-2

**Gran Torino**
Study Guide
10,00 € ◆ / 96 Seiten
ISBN: 978-3-425-04996-0

❑ Wir liefern zur Prüfung mit 20% Nachlass. Gebundener Ladenpreis.
◆ Wir liefern nur an Lehrkräfte, zum vollen Preis, nur ab Verlag.
▼ Unverbindliche Preisempfehlung.

**westermann** GRUPPE

© 2019 Bildungshaus Schulbuchverlage
Westermann Schroedel Diesterweg
Schöningh Winklers GmbH, Braunschweig
www.westermann.de

Druck A[1] / Jahr 2019
Alle Drucke der Serie A sind im Unterricht parallel verwendbar.

Redaktion: Daniel Harnett
Gran Torino Illustrationen: Mario Ellert, Bremen
Umschlagillustration: Jonathan Harris
Layout: Daniel Harnett, Frankfurt am Main
Druck und Bindung: Westermann Druck GmbH, Braunschweig

ISBN 978-3-425-**04977**-9

| | Theme | | Skill |
|---|---|---|---|
| | **1 Identity and belonging** | | |
| 5 | | | Pre-writing |
| | **2 The child** | | |
| 13 | | | Analysis |
| | **3 Gran Torino** | | |
| 23 | | | Characterization |
| | **4 Topics** | | |
| 35 | 4.1 Family | A Fundamental aspects<br>B Focus on belonging<br>C Focus on film and short story | Comment writing |
| 49 | 4.2 The American Dream | A Fundamental aspects<br>B Focus on belonging<br>C Focus on film and short story | Argumentative essay |
| 61 | 4.3 Immigration | A Fundamental aspects<br>B Focus on belonging<br>C Focus on film | Cartoon analysis |
| 73 | 4.4 Race | A Fundamental aspects<br>B Focus on belonging<br>C Focus on short story | Statistics |
| 83 | 4.5 Gun culture | A Fundamental aspects<br>B Focus on belonging<br>C Focus on film | Bilingual dictionary |
| 91 | **5 Wrap up** | | |
| 97 | Portfolio | | |
| 98 | Skills | Statistics<br>Cartoons<br>Comment<br>Pictures<br>Argumentative Essay | |
| 108 | Operators | | |
| 109 | Words | | |
| 120 | Copyrights | | |

Dear students,

This book will help you to prepare for your final exam – the Abitur. In the first module you will find out what *ambiguity of belonging* means, before you start working with the short story *The child* and the film *Gran Torino* in modules two and three. Module four will then introduce you to relevant topics such as *family*, *The American Dream*, *immigration*, *race* and *gun culture*. Across the topics you will also find out what connections can be established with the overall topic of belonging, the short story and the film.

All the best for your preparations and the final exams,

Your *Ambiguity of Belonging* Team

**Gran Torino**

All of the film timings *(Zeitangaben)* refer to the German DVD version of Gran Torino which is available to buy through Westermann (978-3-425-04995-3).

**Audios and Videos**

Throughout the book you will be asked to watch a specific video or listen to an audio file. You will find these files on the following website: **www.diesterweg.de/amb/04977/links**

**Portfolio**

On p. 97 you have space to note down the things you have learnt in each chapter. This could be important vocabulary or expressions you found useful and would like to use more actively in the future, or it could be interesting information about a topic, or it could also be a reminder to yourself to do some extra research into a topic you would like to learn more about.

**1** Describe the pictures.

> **Tip**
> Use the present progressive when describing what people are doing.
> Use the simple present when describing objects and their setting.
> In the first picture there are many … • The fans are watching … •
> In the center of picture three you can see … • Picture four shows five people who are sitting …

**2** a) Many factors help to create a sense of belonging. Which factors are depicted in the pictures above?

_religion_ _____ _____ _____

_____ _____ _____

b) Which other factors can you think of?

_language_ _____ _____ _____

_____ _____ _____

**3** Which factors are important for your sense of belonging? Assign your factors to one of the pictures.

_____ ____ _____ ____ _____ ____

_____ ____ _____ ____ _____ ____

**4** Work with a partner. Explain your choices to each other. Agree on your top three.

**5** Work with the quotes below.

a) Work alone and tick ☑ what you think is the correct version of the quote.

1) **Stephen R. Cowey**
   - ☐ a) I am NOT a product of my circumstances, I AM a product of my decisions.
   - ☐ b) I am NOT a product of my decisions, but I AM a product of my circumstances.

2) **Kurt Cobain**
   - ☐ a) I'd rather be hated for who I am than loved for who I am not.
   - ☐ b) I'd rather be loved for who I am than hated for who I am not.

3) **Rita Mae Brown**
   - ☐ a) The reward for conformity was that everyone liked you except for yourself.
   - ☐ b) The reward for non-conformity was that everyone liked you except for yourself.

4) **Thomas Szarz**
   - ☐ a) The self is not something one finds, it is something ones creates.
   - ☐ b) The self is not something one creates, it is something one finds.

b) Exchange your results with a partner. Justify your opinion by explaining the quote and giving examples.

c) Discuss which quote you agree with the most or the least.

**6** Read the text below.

a) Write down 5 keywords from the text.

b) Exchange your 5 keywords with a partner. Without any preparation time, give a one minute talk on the concept of identity using as many of your partner's keywords as possible.

**The concept of identity**

Have you ever asked yourself "who am I?" or "who do others want me to be?" – The issues of identity encompasses humans all over the world, but the actual concept is hard to understand. Usually identity is defined as the sum of a person's character, beliefs, personality, abilities, interests, experiences and
5 sometimes even of physical appearance; it is influenced by various factors including e.g. our relationships and the environment. Our identity influences the way we see ourselves, what we believe, what we do, how we feel, how we act, and how we interact with people.
However, our sense of identity is far from being static; rather it is a dynamic,
10 ongoing struggle throughout our lives, something that evolves over time as all of us are constantly influenced by circumstances and people around us. Consequently, our thoughts, emotions, attitudes, perspective on ourselves etc. are permanently altered. Depending on who we interact with, we show different facets of our self as we fulfill different roles, e.g. a son, an athlete,
15 a student; depending on the role, different aspects of our identity might surface: one might show off in one's peer group, yet be quite reserved when interacting with one's headmaster or headmistress. This form of amending or even sacrificing parts of one's identity is usually due to our innate desire to belong. Belonging means to feel a sense of being welcomed, supported,
20 accepted and secured as a member or a part. Belonging, respectively not belonging to a certain group of people is the basis of our social status, self-worth and self-esteem. In order to find orientation and to increase our self-esteem we use concepts of otherness and tend to value groups we belong to more than groups we do not belong to.

*to encompass – umfassen*

*struggle – Kampf*
*to evolve – sich entwickeln*

*to alter – ändern*

*to surface – auftauchen*
*to amend – abändern*
*innate – angeboren*

*self-esteem – Selbstwertgefühl*

25 However, negotiating one's sense of self might be problematic due to various reasons; prominent ones are that tensions might arise due to feeling obligated to two conflicting groups (e.g. parents and peers) or feeling torn between one's self-image and the expectations of others (e.g. I want to become a carpenter, but my parents want me to study law).

30 Still, to end on a positive note, one might find consolation in the fact that our identity always being in flux is a natural phenomenon, and that overcoming identity crises helps us to advance in life.

**to negotiate** – *aushandeln; hier: ausloten*
**tensions** – *Spannungen*

**consolation** – *Trost*
**being in flux** – *im Wandel begriffen sein*

**7** Read the text. Then complete the exercises on the next page.

**"The need to belong"**

In their article "The need to belong" psychologists Roy Baumeister and Mark Leary have examined dozens of studies concerning the psychological phenomenon of belonging. One of their findings is that people easily and readily form social bonds and quickly develop a feeling of social attachment.
5 One of the studies that Baumeister and Leary looked at examined how various factors, such as age and interests, influence the formation of relationships. While it is not surprising that many people maintain relationships with their neighbors, it is astonishing that the physical distance between people's homes is a stronger factor than similarities in age or interests. In other words, people
10 are more likely to feel attached to their neighbors than they are to people with similar interests who live further away. Another study shows that people develop positive opinions about people they spend time with, even if these people belong to a group they have disliked before. Psychologists have also discovered that even under adverse conditions such as war, people quickly
15 form social ties.
According to Baumeister and Leary, people do not only easily form relationships, they also have a strong desire to maintain these relationships. In addition, people are reluctant to break social bonds, even if these bonds do not yield obvious advantages. There are countless examples of human
20 behavior which attest to this desire to maintain relationships. Sending Christmas cards to people one hasn't seen in years is such an example. The exchange of greetings and farewells can also be considered proof of people's desire to be accepted and to belong. Even if people end relationships, as in the case of divorce, many of them do not completely cut off all social contact.
25 Baumeister and Leary also claim that there is a clear link between relationships and emotions. Many studies show that forming or strengthening a social bond causes positive emotions. Falling in love is regarded as a typical case of relationship formation, producing intense joy and delight. A marriage is a way of strengthening a social bond, signifying "an increase in commitment
30 to maintaining the relationship permanently [...]." The loss or lack of stable relationships, on the other hand, involves negative feelings. "People who lack belongingness suffer higher levels of mental and physical illness and are relatively highly prone to a broad range of behavioral problems, ranging from traffic accidents to criminality to suicide."
35 In view of all the studies examined by Baumeister and Leary, their claim that "[many] of the strongest emotions people experience, both positive and negative, are linked to belongingness" seems more than justified. They finally remark that "[at] present, it seems fair to conclude that human beings are fundamentally and pervasively motivated by a need to belong, that is, by a
40 strong desire to form and maintain enduring interpersonal attachments."

*(quotes taken from: Roy F. Baumeister, Mark R. Leary, The Need to Belong: Desire for Interpersonal Attachments as a Fundamental Human Motivation, Psychological Bulletin 1995, Vol. 117, No. 3, 497-529)*

**concerning** – *bezüglich*

**to form a social bond** – *eine soziale Bindung eingehen*

**to maintain** – *aufrechterhalten*
**astonishing** – *erstaunlich*

**to feel attached** – *sich verbunden fühlen*

**adverse conditions** – *widrige Umstände*

**desire** – *Wunsch, Bedürfnis*
**to be reluctant to do sth.** – *etw. ungern tun*
**to yield** – *hervorbringen*
**to attest to sth.** – *etw. belegen*
**proof** – *Beweis*

**to claim** – *behaupten*

**commitment** – *Engagement, Verpflichtung*
**lack** – *Mangel, Knappheit*
**to lack sth.** – *etw. nicht haben*
**be prone to sth.** – *zu etw. neigen*

**in view of** – *angesichts*

**justified** – *gerechtfertigt*

a) Read the German expressions and find the highlighted English equivalent in the text on p. 7. There are more highlighted expressions than you need.

| German expression | English equivalent |
|---|---|
| … haben Dutzende von Studien bezüglich … untersucht. | |
| … kann auch als Beleg betrachtet werden für … | |
| … behaupten auch, dass … | |
| … eines ihrer Ergebnisse ist … | |

b) Fill in the gaps with highlighted words and phrases from the text on p. 7. There are more highlighted words and phrases than you need.

1) There are many studies showing that people under adverse conditions are highly motivated

to _____ .

2) According to Baumeister and Leary, _____ leads to positive emotions.

3) Baumeister and Leary looked at a study which shows that many people _____

relationships with their neighbors.

4) According to Baumeister and Leary, there is a clear connection between illnesses and behavioral

problems and  a _____ of _____ .

c) Read the following quotes from the text on p. 7. From what you've experienced in your lifetime, do you agree with the quotes? Write down keywords. Talk to a partner.

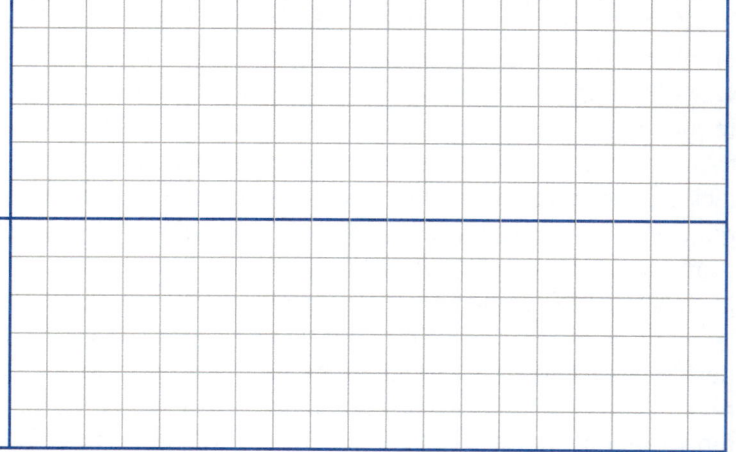

| | |
|---|---|
| a) "One of their findings is that people easily and readily form social bonds and quickly develop a feeling of social attachment." (ll. 3-4) | |
| b) "… people do not only easily form relationships, they also have a strong desire to maintain these relationships." (ll. 16-17) | |

**8** Find out which pre-writing strategy is the best for you. Read the info box on pre-writing activities on p. 9, then do the exercises on p. 10.

## Info box

For your Abitur, you will be asked to write different types of texts. For example, you might have to write a comment, an argumentative essay, a cartoon analysis or a blog entry. Whatever text type you have to produce, it is important that you think about *what* to write and *how* to structure your text beforehand. Pre-writing strategies can help you to generate and to clarify your ideas.

**Brainstorming:** Quickly write down all your thoughts as they come to you. Do not censor yourself while brainstorming. You can evaluate, sort and structure your thoughts in a second step. Many people use bullet points for every new aspect. Therefore brainstorming often looks like a list.

**Clustering/Mind mapping:** This strategy helps you to explore relationships between ideas. Put one word or a short phrase in the center of a page and circle or underline it. Write down related terms, ideas, concepts etc. you associate with the central subject and connect them to each other.

**Free writing:** Set yourself a time limit, let your thoughts flow and write everything down that comes into your mind. Do not stop writing to think but keep writing. You can sort and structure your thoughts afterwards. If you don't know what to write, then write down something like "What else can I write about …". For the task "Write a paragraph for your blog about the following statement: Belonging causes positive feelings" your pre-writing could look like this.

**Example Brainstorming:**

- *Baumeister and Leary*
- *falling in love*
- *stable family*
- *break ups hurt*

- *When you belong you feel:  happy, content, safe, confident*
- *good friends*
- *creates value in life*

**Example Clustering/Mind mapping:**

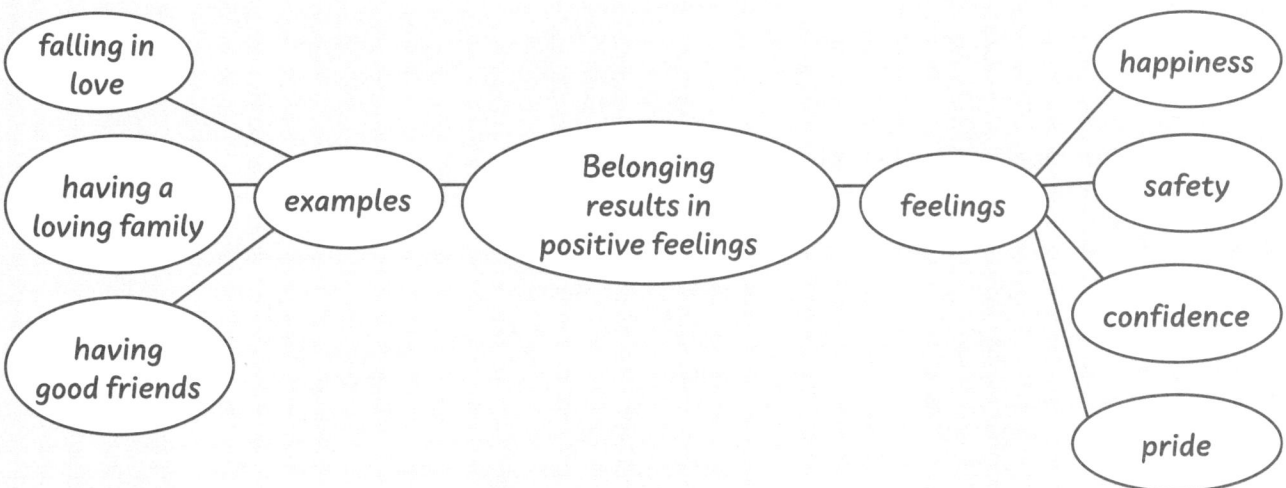

**Example Free writing:**

*Yes, belonging does cause positive feelings. When you fall in love with someone you feel very happy and content and nothing can make you feel sad. What are other positive feelings that people have when they belong? I cannot think of positive feelings. Ah, they might feel secure or even confident. What else could I write about the topic? I could write about examples of belonging like when you are part of a group of friends or part of a happy family. It is also interesting to look at people who do not have a feeling of belonging. They are normally depressed and have a lot of negative feelings.*

a) Use the strategy brainstorming to plan the following task:
Write a paragraph about the following statement *"People easily form social bonds."*

b) Use the strategy clustering/mind mapping to plan the following task:
Write a paragraph about the following statement *"People want to maintain social bonds."*

c) Use the strategy free writing to plan the following task:
Write a paragraph about the following statement *"Not belonging causes pain."*

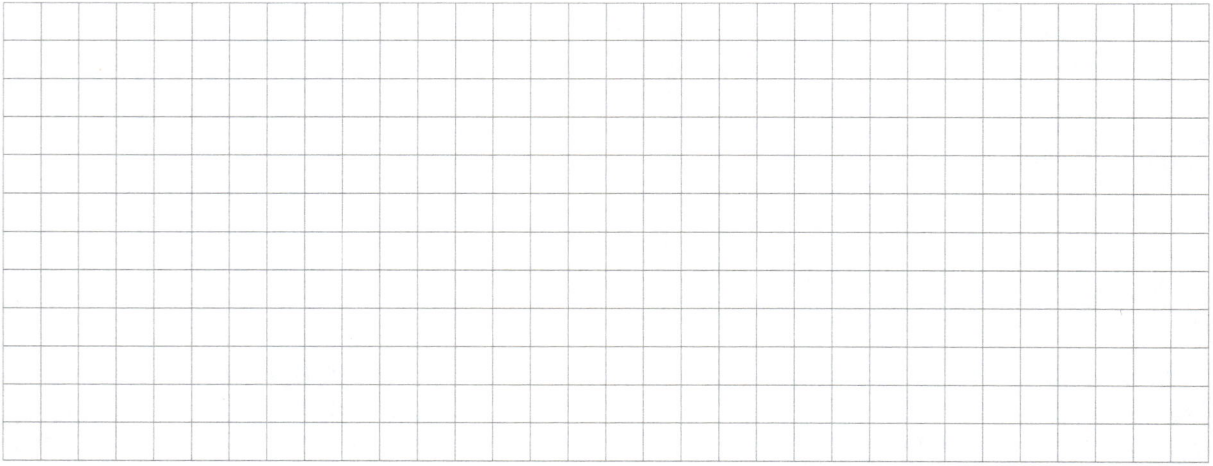

d) Talk to your partner about which strategy works best for you.

e) Write the paragraph for one of the tasks.

**9** a) Complete the table below using the words from the box.

> unclear, vague, confusing • one feels at least two ways about something • used to describe things or things people do and say • something can be understood in at least two different ways (open to interpretation) • mixed feelings/attitudes, contradictory ideas • used to describe a person, feelings, attitudes, relationships

| ambiguous *(mehrdeutig)* | ambivalent *(zwiespältig)* |
|---|---|
| "The book has an ambiguous ending." | "She is ambivalent about going to the party." |
| *unclear, vague, confusing* | |
| | |
| | |

**Both may, but do not necessarily have to result in a state of**
**being unsure** *(sich nicht sicher sein)*/**insecure** *(sich unsicher fühlen)*.

b) Read the following sentences and decide whether *ambiguous* or *ambivalent* has to be used. Cross out the incorrect one.

1) The result of the study is ambiguous/ambivalent.

2) The girl gave him an ambiguous/ambivalent look.

3) The public tends to have an ambiguous/ambivalent attitude regarding privacy.

4) The new law is written in an ill-defined, ambiguous/ambivalent way.

5) He had been ambiguous/ambivalent about his maleness but he made peace with it.

6) If you are ambiguous/ambivalent about ambiguous/ambivalent films, stay away from them.

**10** a) Have a look at the following quotes. Talk to a partner. Use the terms *ambivalence/ambivalent* or *ambiguity/ambiguous* to describe what they tell you about the feeling of belonging.

1
Friends from college are fairly important to me. But when I come back home to my family and neighborhood I feel that I talk and act differently.

2
I do love my mates. But sometimes they make me join in activities I kind of disapprove of.

3
My parents move quite frequently. I'd rather stay in one place. I sometimes get the impression that I rarely know where my home is.

b) Think of other situations where the feeling of belonging might be ambiguous, where people might feel ambivalent, or where something is ambiguous. Note them down.

c) Write an additional paragraph for the text on p. 7 focusing on the ambiguity of belonging.

**1**  The title of the short story you are going to read is *The child*. Use the title to speculate on the content of this short story. The expressions in the box may help you.

> The story might revolve around … •  I would imagine that the story … •
> The title suggests that the story / the story's protagonist … •  I expect a story about …

**2**  Look very closely at the photo below and describe it in as much detail as possible. Pay attention to the surroundings, the people and their genders, ages, clothes, facial expressions etc.

**3**  a) Read the first three paragraphs of the story (up to line 29). Decide what type of story *The child* is going to be: a crime story, a romance, a detective story, a tragedy, an adventure story, a parody/satire, a fantasy or a coming-of-age story.

b) Take a closer look at the first three paragraphs and highlight passages that serve as evidence for your decision.

c) Discuss your decision with a partner. Use the following expressions in your discussion.

> We can take … as a hint that the story is a … •  … indicates that it might be a … story. •
> The fact that Karen … suggests that the story may develop into a … story.

**4**  Read the whole story. Then talk about the following questions with a partner:

- Are there any aspects that you haven't understood?
- What aspects would you like to look at in more detail?
- Now that you have read the complete short story, what genre does the story belong to?

# The child
*by Julius Lester*

Gently, Karen went down the steps to the subway, flashed[1] her student pass at the attendant in the token booth[2], and walked through the gate onto the platform. It was morning, though one did not know
5 that beneath the ground. But Karen had not paid much attention to the day before descending the steps stained by traces of urine, wine, soda, cigarette butts and wrappers[3] torn from candy bars[4]. She looked up the track even though she knew the vibrations of the
10 train would be felt and heard before seeing the light from its far-reaching beam[5]. It was something to do, and she needed something to do this morning.

She was small and looked younger than her seventeen years. Being neither prettier nor uglier
15 than any girl that age, there was nothing memorable about her. If anyone standing in the subway station had thought to focus attention upon her (and no one did), they might have noticed that she was standing dangerously close to the edge, as if she would not
20 have minded if a breeze or hand had pushed her onto the tracks. They also would have noticed that, unlike the other teenagers waiting for the train, no book bag hung lazily from her shoulder giving a sense of purposefulness. In her jeans and white blouse and
25 with her empty hands, Karen seemed to be without destination or function. But no one noticed.

*"I used to be a fighter. Ha! Ha! That's the truth! I fought Muhammed Ali[6] and beat'im! I whupped him so bad they made me quit the ring! Ha! Ha! Ha!"*

30 She turned and stared at the drunk man who had just staggered[7] through the turnstile[8], spit dribbling from a corner of his mouth and down his chin. His brown face was caked with dirt mixed with dried blood. His clothes reminded her of the subway station steps,
35 and she moved even closer to the edge and peered up the track again. She wondered why she cared if the train ever came. Where was she going to go?

She hadn't really expected her mother to believe she was just putting on weight, not she who was as thin
40 as sorrow.

"Girl, what is the matter with you? You think I be working two jobs and praying all the time, for you to go get yourself knocked up[9] the first time a boy look at you and say hi? Help me, Jesus! Help me!"

45 "Ain't nothing he can do, Mama."

"How would you know? If you had had your mind on Jesus, you wouldn't be in this condition. How could you let something like this happen?"

"You see, Mama, it was like this. You go up on the
50 roof on a warm night and you see the cutest boy that has ever walked the earth and somebody has a radio and you get to talking and somebody else has a little smoke and somewhere between the sweet words and the sweet music and the sweet smoke,
55 he touches you, and, Mama, I never felt a feeling like that feeling when a boy touches you here and there, and there and here. Mama, I would do anything to feel like that *all the time*. You understand me, Mama. I would do anything to feel like that all the time. But
60 it got even better than that. Yes, it did, Mama. But I don't be having to explain none of this to you, now do I, Mama? Wasn't you about seventeen when you had me?"

That was when her mother slapped her.[10]

65 Karen slapped her back.

Now she got ready to board the subway as she felt the push of hot air through the tunnel signaling its coming even before the light shone down the track or the walls trembled.

70 *"Hold that door! If you don't I'll kick your behind like I done Ali!"*

When the train rumbled into the station, the doors slid open and people pushed their way off and on at the same time. Karen waited, afraid someone would
75 brush against her, afraid they would hurt the first thing in her life she could call her own.

She was surprised when no one offered her a seat. Couldn't they tell? She was different now. She wasn't like them. Couldn't they tell she was going to be a
80 mother?

---

**Annotations:**
[1] **to flash sth. at sb.** = to quickly show sb. sth.;
[2] **token booth** = *Fahrkartenschalter*; [3] **wrapper** = *Verpackung*;
[4] **candy bar** (AE) = chocolate bar; [5] **beam** = line of light;
[6] **Muhammad Ali (1942-2016)** = famous African American boxer,
considered one of the greatest athletes of the 20th century;
[7] **to stagger** = to walk unsteadily; [8] **turnstile** = *Drehkreuz*;
[9] **to get knocked up (coll.)** = to become pregnant;
[10] **to slap sb.** = to hit sb. with a flat hand

The train lurched[11] forward, and she leaned against the door between the cars. She wanted to shout and tell everyone to look at her. She was going to be a mother! But she was afraid that if she yelled[12], no one
85 would hear. All her life she had felt like something happened to the words between the time they left her lips and went toward other people's ears. Was there an invisible thief who stole words from the mouths of girls, leaving them to wonder if they had spoken,
90 leaving them to wonder if they really existed? She had lived for seventeen years and never seen anybody's eyes come alive when she walked into a room. She had lived for seventeen years, and her existence had never put a smile on anybody's face. She had lived for
95 seventeen years, and no one had noticed.

Then Philip had looked at her, and suddenly it mattered to someone that she was alive and not dead. He made her feel that the sun rose over her head and set at her feet. When he looked at her, she
100 felt pretty. She wasn't and she knew it, but what did that have to do with anything? He held her; he touched her; he made her feel so good that she didn't know what she wanted the most – to live or to die.

When she told him she thought she was pregnant, he
105 was happy. He laughed and strutted[13] up and down like he had just won the lottery. She was relieved he wasn't going to make her get rid of it like Darlene's boyfriend had done her. But when she asked him to go with her to the hospital for the test, he said
110 just because he got her pregnant didn't mean he was going to be a daddy, and he wasn't about to be nobody's husband. He laughed again, and she understood that what was growing inside of her wasn't anything to him but proof of his manhood.

115 *"Anybody want to fight? Huh? Anybody want to fight?"*

There was that ol' drunk man, hanging on to a strap[14] for dear life as the train swayed from side to side. The least he could do was wipe the spit from his chin and stop disgracing[15] every black person on the subway
120 car.

Karen didn't want her child exposed to someone like him, not even while it was in the womb.[16] Not her baby! She turned her eyes away and noticed a white girl seated in the middle of the car. She had long dark
125 hair that spilled over her shoulders like silk threads.

A book was open on her lap. Karen wished she could have hated her. Instead, she wanted to ask her what she was reading and what it was about. She wanted to smooth[17] her hair and see if it was as soft as it
130 looked. She wanted to go home with her and see the pictures on her walls and the color of the spread[18] on her bed. Most of all, she wanted to hear her dreams. Not the ones that came in the night, unbidden and unwanted, but the ones that came when you were
135 standing in the shower or walking along a street with nothing on your mind, or when you were sitting on the subway trying hard not to look at anybody.

*"Y'all scared, ain't ya? You better be. I'll whup yo' head for you."*

140 Karen could not imagine dreams stretching from one side of the sky to the other, dreams that spun[19] themselves because that was what dreams were supposed to do like waves were supposed to arch and curl and fall. She wondered if you needed clean,
145 quiet streets and big rooms and two parents who you knew in order to dream. She wondered if you needed white skin.

None of that mattered now. It would be a while before she read another schoolbook, what with
150 the baby due[20] in March. She wanted to believe she would go back and finish after the baby came, but none of her friends who'd had babies had done that. But that was okay. Seventeen years from next spring, her baby would finish school for both of them.

155 Her child wasn't going to have nothing to do with winos[21] and junkies and dirty streets and loud music. It would stay inside and read big books and be real smart, and when it got grown, it would say, "Mama, let's go. I'm going to move you out of here. I'm going
160 to take you away from all these drunk people and junkies."

Karen started to smile. Then she stopped, wondering suddenly if this new dream of hers had been her own mother's dream for the past seventeen years.
165 *Oh, Mama!* she exclaimed to herself. *I'm so sorry.* She wanted to cry, but what good would it do?

Her mother shouldn't have had dreams for her, just like she shouldn't be having dreams for her baby. Everybody had to find their own dreams.

**Annotations:**
[11] **to lurch** = to move suddenly; [12] **to yell** = to shout; [13] **to strut** = to walk proudly; [14] **strap** = piece of plastic or leather that you hold on to on a bus or subway; [15] **to disgrace sb.** = to do harm to sb.'s or a group's reputation by doing sth. bad; [16] **womb** = part of a woman's body that a child grows in; [17] **to smooth** = *glätten*; [18] **spread** = cover of a bed; [19] **to spin, span, spun** = to turn around and around; [20] **due** = having a fixed date when sth. will happen; [21] **wino (coll.)** = alcoholic

170 Her mother had been happier than Karen was when she had been accepted at the High School for Fashion and Design. "My daughter is going to be somebody!" her mother had exclaimed.

Be who? Karen wondered. Be what? Just because she 175 could draw clothes didn't mean she was going to be a big fashion designer. If she had been white, like that girl, if her hair had been as smooth as a cloudless sky, then she would have dreamed. But it didn't pay to be black and to dream. It didn't pay. What happened to 180 you when the dream didn't come true? What did you do then?

She looked at the white girl robed in her straight hair. That girl was somebody just because. That was the same reason Karen wasn't.

185 Karen touched her stomach lightly. It didn't feel any different. It was hard to believe a person was inside. Well, maybe not a person like she was, but it would be.

The train stopped. Before Karen could get a seat, a group of white boys yelled and shouted their way 190 onto the coach[22], pushing each other playfully for the few empty seats.

*"You kids watch whar you goin'. I do you like I done Ali."*

"Yeah! That's right, old man!"

"You tell us about it!"

195 "Ha! Ha! Ha!"

Those kids didn't have no right to be making fun of him like that. Couldn't they tell there was something wrong with him? Whatever made him like that wasn't all his fault. Yet Karen said nothing aloud and 200 wished that ol' drunk fool would get off the train and stop embarrassing her. Didn't he know that white people judged all black people by how each of them behaved? Somebody in his life must have told him that. Didn't he have any pride in himself and his race?

205 *"You think cause you white you can mess with me. Let me tell you one thing. One of these days you gon' be sorry."*

"We'll be sorry as you! Right? HaHaHa!"

Her child was going to be a credit to[23] the race. Like 210 her, she added glumly[24]. Well, having a baby wasn't the end of the world. People had babies every day. It wasn't no big deal. Not really. At least she had something to do with herself now. She was going to be the best mama anybody had ever seen. She was 215 going to love this baby until it begged for mercy.

*"Make fun of me if you want to, but I know what I'm talking 'bout. You think I'm drunk. I ain't as much drunk as you is 'sleep."*

Karen looked at the white girl. Through all the yelling 220 between the old man and the boys, she had not raised her head from her book. Karen doubted that she had heard – and why should she have? It wasn't like the old man could've been her father or grandfather. He was just an old black man to her. Maybe not even that.

225 Was that what it was like to be white? That you didn't have to care about anybody except yourself? You didn't even have to think about anybody else. You could sit on the subway and not even notice other white people and what they did. You didn't have to 230 worry about what people might be thinking about you because somebody white was drunk or passed out[25] from drugs. She shook her head, unable to imagine what it would be like to be free of other people's thoughts and opinions and ideas about you.

235 Karen gazed[26] enviously[27] at the white girl, wondering what her boyfriend was like and if he made her feel good. But her boyfriend would not have laughed at her if she was going to have his baby.

She touched her stomach again. Everything will be 240 all right, she said silently to it. *It'll take a while, but everything will work out. I'll go back to school next fall and finish up and design clothes for little babies like you. And one day I'll go see Mama, and I'll be driving a big car and I'll say, "'Bye, Mama," and I'll drive over the 245 George Washington Bridge. I'll turn on the radio, and it'll be on all the news: "Miss Karen Bridges left New York City today on her way to Hollywood where she will become the dress designer for the stars."*

That was how it would be. One day.

250 And she turned her back because she didn't want the girl to look up from the book and see her crying.

---

**Annotations:**
[22] **coach** = a car of a train
[23] **to be a credit to sb./sth.** = jdm./etw. Ehre machen
[24] **glum** = depressed
[25] **to be passed out** = to be unconscious
[26] **to gaze** = to look at sb./sth. for a long time
[27] **envious** = wanting what sb. else has

**5** The following reactions are taken from an online forum where readers discuss literature. Having now read the story, discuss these reactions in groups of three.

A friend of mine told me to read *The child* by Julius Lester. I have read a lot of novels and short stories in my life, mostly detective fiction and romances, and I was a bit disappointed, especially with the ending. I don't think I would recommend the story to anyone.

*John "Sherlock" Kennedy*

I also read *The child* and I agree with Sherlock that it's not good entertainment. Where are the characters I can identify with? Where is the suspense? Where is the action?

*Rachel Reader*

**6** Go back to the short story and decide which of these statements are true or false. Give evidence using keywords and include line references.

| | true | false | evidence |
|---|---|---|---|
| a) The conversation between Karen and her mother takes place in the subway station. | | | |
| b) The white girl on the subway has short, curly hair. | | | |
| c) Karen is envious of the white girl. | | | |
| d) Karen and Philip met at the High School for Fashion and Design. | | | |
| e) The reason why Karen finds the old man's behaviour so embarrassing is that he is also an African American. | | | |

**7**   Look at the following words and phrases. Then choose appropriate ones for each character.

> to be afraid of sth.  •  ambitious *(ehrgeizig)*  •  angry  •  anxious *(besorgt)*  •  to be ashamed of sth.  •  black  •
> caring  •  charming  •  cheerful  •  confident  •  desperate *(verzweifelt)*  •  determined *(entschlossen)*  •
> disappointed  •  envious *(neidisch)*  •  furious *(wütend)*  •  hopeful  •  hurt  •  impatient  •  impulsive  •
> irresponsible  •  lonely  •  to feel miserable  •  naive  •  neglected *(vernachlässigt)*  •  optimistic  •
> to be proud of sth.  •  rebellious  •  sensitive *(sensibel)*  •  shabby  •  shy  •  to have straight hair  •
> successful  •  to wear jeans  •  white  •  young

|  | Karen | her mother | Philip | drunk man | white girl |
|---|---|---|---|---|---|
| outward appearance |  |  |  |  |  |
| emotional state |  |  |  |  |  |

**8**   Fill in the grid. In the second column, note down the name of the character the quote refers to. In the third column, note down what the quote reveals about the character.

| quote | character | what it reveals |
|---|---|---|
| a) "She hadn't really expected her mother to believe she was just putting on weight" (ll. 38-39) |  |  |
| b) "I used to be a fighter. Ha! Ha! That's the truth! I fought Muhammad Ali and beat'im!" (ll. 27-28) |  |  |
| c) "He laughed and strutted up and down like he had just won the lottery." (ll. 105-106) |  |  |
| d) "She touched her stomach again." (l. 239) |  |  |

| | | |
|---|---|---|
| e) "he made her feel so good that she didn't know what she wanted the most" (ll. 102-103) | | |
| f) "Help me, Jesus! Help me!" (l. 44) | | |
| g) "She was surprised when no one offered her a seat." (l. 77) | | |

**9** a) Use the arrows below to show the relationships between the characters. Use each arrow only once.

b) Discuss why you chose to place the arrows where you did.

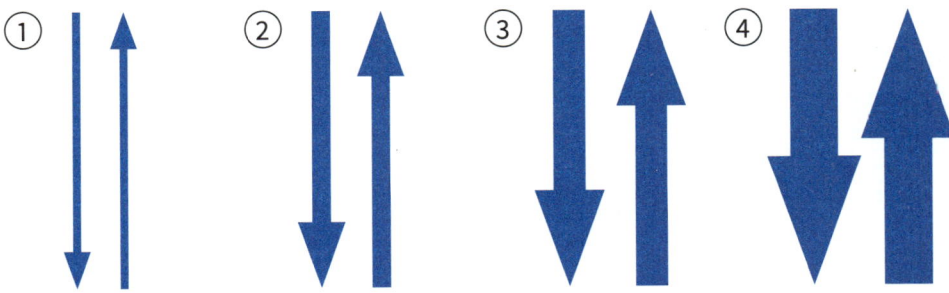

Karen's mother

the white girl    KAREN    Philip

the drunk man

**10** a) During the course of the story, Karen undergoes different emotional states. Use the quotes below to explain these states. The order of the quotes is the same as in the story. The words and phrases from task 7 may help you.

| quote | explanation |
|---|---|
| 1) "He made her feel that the sun rose over her head and set at her feet." | *Karen is in love for the first time and Philip gives her the feeling that she is the centre of the world. She feels loved and desired.* |
| 2) "He laughed again, and she understood that what was growing inside of her wasn't anything to him but proof of his manhood." | |
| 3) "She wanted to shout and tell everyone to look at her. She was going to be a mother!" | |
| 4) "Karen didn't want her child exposed to someone like him, not even while it was in the womb. Not her baby!" | |
| 5) "She wondered if you needed clean, quiet streets and big rooms and two parents who you knew in order to dream." | |
| 6) "She wanted to believe she would go back and finish after the baby came, but none of her friends who'd had babies had done that." | |
| 7) "'Mama, let's go. I'm going to move you out of here.'" | |
| 8) "*Oh, Mama!* she exclaimed to herself. *I'm so sorry.*" | |
| 9) "If she had been white, like that girl, if her hair had been as smooth as a cloudless sky, then she would have dreamed." | |
| 10) "Her child was going to be a credit to the race." | |
| 11) "That was how it would be. One day. And she turned her back because she didn't want the girl to look up from the book and see her crying." | |

b) Use your results from a) to draw a line that represents Karen's emotional states.

optimistic

pessimistic

plot: beginning                                                        plot: end

**11** a) Read the text of *The child* again (pp. 14-16) and then highlight the passages that contain information about the plot and that tell us what Karen does. Then, using a different color, highlight the passages which tell us what Karen is thinking.

b) Examine the result and note down your findings in one or two sentences.

**12** a) Read the following passage from *The child* and the descriptions of narrative techniques. Then match the techniques to the three parts of the passage.

| 1. The narrator assumes a character's perspective and communicates his or her thoughts and feelings. | 2. A character's thoughts and feelings are communicated to the reader directly without tags like "she thought" or "she said to herself." This mode is called free indirect style. | 3. The narrator looks at things from outside of the narrative and tells the reader what is happening. |
|---|---|---|

| quote | narrative technique |
|---|---|
| When the train rumbled into the station, the doors slid open and people pushed their way off and on at the same time. | |
| Karen waited, afraid someone would brush against her, afraid they would hurt the first thing in her life she could call her own. She was surprised when no one offered her a seat. | |
| Couldn't they tell? She was different now. She wasn't like them. Couldn't they tell she was going to be a mother? | |

b) Explain the effects that are achieved by the different modes of narration chosen by the narrator in the passage above. Use at least five of the following words and phrases.

a character's mind • to feel sympathy for • to learn something about a character •
to reduce the distance between … and … • to have access to • the inner life of a character • reality

c) Explain how you would turn this passage into a film scene.

**13**   a) Explain what effect Karen's pregnancy has on her. Think about both the practical and the psychological aspects. Use at least five of the ten following phrases.

> As a consequence, Karen … • For the first time in her life, Karen … • her unborn child •
> to have hopes for sb. • to protect sb. • a purpose in life • to have ambivalent feelings •
> to make plans • to be pregnant • to think of friends who have babies

b) "Karen is happy to be pregnant." Comment on this statement.

    📖 **How to write a comment → see skills pp. 102-103**

**14** **Choose**

Write a letter to Karen from Philip's perspective. He wants to explain his feelings concerning her pregnancy.

**OR**

Write a letter to Philip from Karen's perspective. She wants to explain her situation.

**15** Go back to Rachel Reader's comment on *The child* in task 5. Write the answer you would post to her comment on the online literary forum.

## A – Fundamental aspects

**1** Underline the skills, ideas, qualities and objects in the box below that are typically and traditionally mentioned in connection with masculinity.

> a sense of independence • conversations about feelings and anxieties *(Befürchtungen, Ängste)* • asking others for help • the skill to maintain *(erhalten)* and repair your possessions *(Eigentum)* • self-reliance *(Eigenständigkeit)* • reluctance *(Abneigung)* to talk about emotions • cars and trucks • negotiating compromises *(Kompromisse aushandeln)* • the ability to provide for a family *(für eine Familie sorgen)* • solving problems by using tools, weapons, physical strength

**2** Compare your results with a partner, then talk about each picture using the underlined words and expressions.

**3** The following statements were uttered by John Wayne, one of the most famous American actors who starred in dozens of Western movies.

*"A man's got to do what a man's got to do."*

*"I'm not the sort to back away from a fight. I don't believe in shrinking from anything. It's not my speed; I'm a guy who meets adversities head on."*

The quotes as well as the pictures also refer to qualities that are typically associated with white American men. Use your knowledge of American history and relate the quotes and pictures to specific events and developments.

*Example: When the first settlers arrived in the New World, they were confronted with lots of challenges and had to solve the problems on their own by using the tools they had such as weapons.*

**Psychology Today**
**Do White Males Feel They Are Losing Their "Space?"**
*Rosalind C. Barnett, Ph.D., and Caryl Rivers*                    *4 January 2019*

*Men are facing new anxieties*

Do many white American men feel that their "space" is disappearing with the new demographics of America? Do we hear echoes of the anxiety caused by the closing of the frontier in 1890, when the U.S. census decreed that the
5 frontier no longer existed?
At that time, historian Frederick Turner reacted with alarm, because he believed that the open, seemingly limitless frontier with all its freedoms formed the rugged American character. He worried that American dynamism and energetic masculinity would vanish along with the frontier.
10 Henry James echoed this sentiment in his novel of the same era, *The Bostonians*: "The whole generation is womanized; the masculine tone is passing out of the world; it's a feminine, a nervous, hysterical, chattering, canting age, an age of hollow phrases and false delicacy and exaggerated solicitudes and coddled sensibilities."
15 Today's closing frontier is not a geographical space but a psychological one. Ever since the founding of the nation, white men – especially straight white Christian men – have been in charge. They have been our presidents, our captains of industry, our generals, our Wall Street titans, and they held all the power. They were the ones in "The room where it happens," as the *Hamilton*
20 lyric observes.
Even men who had no wealth or celebrity or grand accomplishments could bask in the glow of white male hegemony. They could at least imagine themselves in those "happening" rooms because all the people there looked like them.
25 We (a researcher and a journalist) have been following the narrative of male anxiety for four decades, and we have seen the ebb and flow of such fears. Today, we believe, the anxiety is at fever pitch, fanned by the incendiary words of President Donald Trump. More than 60,000 psychologists and other mental health professionals signed a petition titled *Duty to Warn*, saying that
30 the nation is in peril because of Trump's mental Instability. He is exacerbating the male fear of "losing space" in today's world. […]

| | |
|---|---|
| **anxiety** | – *Angst* |
| **frontier** | – the (imaginary) line between what the settlers regarded civilization and wilderness during the conquest of the American continent |
| **to decree** | – *beschließen* |
| **Fredrick Turner** | – famous American historian |
| **rugged** | – *kräftig, rau* |
| **to vanish** | – *verschwinden* |
| **sentiment** | – *Ansicht, Meinung* |
| **canting** | – *scheinheilig* |
| **delicacy** | – *Empfindsamkeit* |
| **to coddle** | – *verhätscheln* |
| **hollow** | – *hohl* |
| **solicitude** | – *Besorgtheit* |
| **straight** | – *hier: heterosexuell* |
| **accomplishment** | – *Leistung* |
| **to bask in the glow** | – *sich im Glanz sonnen* |
| **narrative** | – *Erzählung* |
| **the ebb and flow** | – *das Auf und Ab* |
| **to be at fever pitch** | – *sich am Siedepunkt befinden* |
| **incendiary** | – *aufwiegelnd* |
| **petition** | – *Unterschriftenliste* |
| **in peril** | – *in Gefahr* |
| **to exacerbate** | – *verschlimmern* |

**4**   According to the authors of the text above, many white males in the U.S. currently feel they are "losing space" – they are losing the world they used to belong to.

a) Write down what this world was like according to the authors.

_____

_____

_____

b) Speculate about the reasons why many white Americans have, at least partially, lost their sense of belonging. Look at the following terms and decide which of them might have contributed to male anxieties.

digitalization · feminism · climate change · inequality between poor and rich · immigration · outsourcing

**Part 1: Watch the movie up to 27:32**

**5** a) Choose from the list of adjectives below those which describes the image of Walt as conveyed in the film stills and quotes best.

> reluctant *(zögerlich)* • self-reliant *(selbständig, auf sich selbst verlassen)* • considerate *(rücksichtsvoll)* • conscience-stricken *(schuldbewusst)* • practical • considerate *(rücksichtsvoll)* • determined *(entschlossen)* • with a positive outlook on life • lonely

8:45

24:38

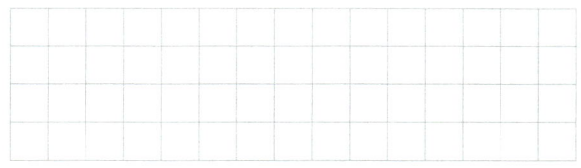

*Scene with Walt Kowalski's grandsons in the basement of his house.*

*Scene in the living room.*

**DAVID**
Is that Dad?
**DANIEL**
No, it's Grandpa Walt.

*Josh turns the photo over and reads it...*

**JOSH**
'Third Platoon, E company, March second, 1952, Korea.'

**ASHLEY**
Grandpa Walt, would you like some help with this, with the chairs?
**WALT**
No, you probably just painted your nails.

b) Use the pictures and quotes above in order to find out whether Walt Kowalski can be interpreted as a typical American white man. Refer to your findings from p. 23.

**6**    a) Compare Walt Kowalski's property and his neighbor's property. Write down the statements next to the film still. Use expressions from the box.

> Walt's … is … compared to his neighbor's … •  Unlike his neighbor's house, his house … •
> While Walt's property looks …, his neighbor's property  •  Walt seems to …,  whereas his neighbors … •
> In contrast to his neighbors, he …

*Walt's property has a driveway, whereas his neighbor's house doesn't.*

b) Use your results from 6a), the excerpts from the film script below and on the next page, as well as other scenes from the movie to analyze what happened to Walt's sense of belonging. Write down keywords, then exchange your results with a partner.

*Scene in which Walt Kowalski and Phong meet for the first time.*

> **WALT**
> Jesus, Polarski would roll over in his grave if he could see his lawn now. What the hell did Chinks have to move into this neighborhood for?
> **PHONG**
> Why does that old white man stay here? All the Americans have moved out of this neighborhood.

*Scene when Walt's son Mitch and his family leave the funeral reception.*

*Mitch, Karen, Ashley and Josh pull up next to Walt in a brand new Toyota Land Cruiser. Mitch opens the window.*

**MITCH**
I'd really like to help, Dad, but we have to get the kids home, they're getting restless.
Walt just looks at the TOYOTA EMBLEM on the Land Cruiser and then gives Mitch a disgusted glance.
**WALT**
Fine. Go.
**MITCH**
I'll call in a few, see how you're doing.

*Walt nods and lights a cigarette as they drive off.*

**WALT**
Kill you to buy American.
**MITCH**
Did you see him look at the truck? It's always Rice-Burner this or Jap-Buggy that. Even at Mom's funeral, he can't let it go.
**KAREN**
At least he didn't say anything this time.
**MITCH**
He didn't have to.
**KAREN**
Well, what do you expect? The man worked at a Ford plant for twenty-eight years.

**7** Read the following text.

## Info Box : Why we insult others

No one seriously questions the thesis that, by and large, humans want to get along well with each other. We are all social beings in need of positive relationships. In fact, every successful society is largely based on the principle of cooperation. At the same time people quite often insult each other on purpose. Decades of research shows that there is probably much truth in the widely held belief that people insult others in order to feel better about themselves.

A lot of insulting behavior can be traced back to threatened self-esteem, according to researchers. This phenomenon can be observed both in people who are generally happy with themselves as well as in people with a low self-esteem. Whenever people feel worse about themselves than they usually do, they are more prone to insult others.

Another reason why people insult others is our desire to belong to groups. According to proponents of social identity theory one way of strengthening the bond with our in-group (the group we want to belong to) is by ridiculing or insulting other groups. This pattern or principle can often be observed when there is competition between the groups or when people fear their identity or the identity of their group is challenged.

**to insult** – *beleidigen*

**to question** – *infrage stellen*

**on purpose** – *mit Absicht*
**widely held belief** – *weit verbreitete Ansicht*

**self-esteem** – *Selbstwertgefühl*
**to be prone to do sth.** – *dazu neigen, etw. zu tun*

**proponent** – *Vertreter*

**to ridicule** – *verspotten*
**pattern** – *Muster*

**8**   Complete the sentences below. Use the information from the info box.

a) People insult each other even though _____

_____

b) People insult each other when _____

_____

c) People insult each other in order to _____

_____

**9**   *"It may be the case that Walt's self-esteem is threatened and that he fears the loss of everything he has held dear throughout his life, but that's not why he insults others. He does this because he is a moody, bad-tempered racist."*

Discuss the given statement. Bear in mind what you know about the world of white males and about insulting language.

| Yes, I agree / arguments in favour … | I disagree / arguments against … |
| --- | --- |
| | |

**10**   Summarize the first part of the movie (up to 27:32). Use your knowledge from tasks 1 – 9 as well as the vocabulary provided in the boxes.

*In the first part of "Gran Torino", Walt Kowalksi is shown as a grumpy old man who*

**Part 2: Watch the movie from 27:32 to 1:16:45**

**11** The following scenes are the first conversations between Walt Kowalski and Father Janovich. Analyze the conversation bearing in mind what you know about Walt's sense of belonging. Pay special attention to the way the characters use language. Fill in the table below.

*The first encounter between Walt Kowalski and Father Janovich, at Mrs. Kowalki's funeral.*

**FATHER JANOVICH**
How you holding up, Walt?
**WALT**
Mr. Kowalski.
**FATHER JANOVICH**
Huh?
**WALT**
It's Mr. Kowalski, not Walt.
**FATHER JANOVICH**
Right, Mr. Kowalski. Your wife and I became quite close these last few months. She asked that I watch over you when she passed on. I told her I watch out for my entire flock, but she made me promise I'd keep an extra sharp eye on you.

**WALT**
I appreciate your kindness to my wife and now that you've spoken your piece, why don't you move on to the next sheep?

[…]

**WALT**
Well, I confess I never much liked church and only went because of the wife. And I confess I have no desire to confess to a boy who is fresh out of the seminary.

| What Father Janovich says | Father Janovich's intention | How he tries to achieve his aim |
|---|---|---|
| *How you holding up, Walt?* | *He wants to get in touch with Walt.* | *He uses informal language (holding up) and he addresses Walt by his first name.* |

| What Walt says | Walt's intention | How he tries to achieve his aim |
|---|---|---|
|  |  |  |

**12** The following scene is the third conversation between Father Janovich and Walt Kowalski. Analyze the conversation, bearing in mind what you know of Walt's sense of belonging.

**FATHER JANOVICH**
Good afternoon, Walt.
**WALT**
I told you I'm not going to confession…
**FATHER JANOVICH**
Why didn't you just call the police?
**WALT**
What?
**FATHER JANOVICH**
I do work with some of the Hmong gangs and I heard there was some trouble in the neighborhood. Why didn't you call the police?
**WALT**
Well … You know why, I've prayed that they would show up, but … nobody answered.
**FATHER JANOVICH**
What were you thinking? Someone could have been killed. We're talking life and death here.
**WALT**
When things go wrong, you gotta act quickly. When we were in Korea and a thousand screaming gooks came across our land … we didn't call the police. We reacted.
**FATHER JANOVICH**
We are not in Korea, Mr. Kowalski, I've been thinking about our conversation on life and death.

About what you said. About how you carry around all the horrible things you were forced to do Horrible things that won't leave you. It seems that it would do you good to unload some of that burden. Things done during war are terrible. being ordered to kill … killing to save yourself, killing to save others. You're right, those are things I know nothing about. But I do know about forgiveness. And I've seen a lot of men who have confessed their sins, admitted their guilt and left their burdens behind them. Stronger men than you! Men at war who were ordered to do appalling things … and are now at peace.
**WALT**
Well I got to hand it to you, padre, you came here with your guns loaded this time. Thank you! – And you're right about one thing. About stronger men than me, reaching their salvation. Well, Hallefuckinlujah. – But you are wrong about something else.
**FATHER JANOVICH**
What's that, Mr. Kowalski?
**WALT**
The thing that haunts a man the most is what he isn't ordered to do.

**13** Describe in what ways their relationship has changed. Use expressions from 6a) (p. 26)

**14** a) Use the two film stills below to compare Walt's family with the Hmong family.
Talk about the following aspects:

- relationships between younger and older family members
- traditions and customs
- values and principles

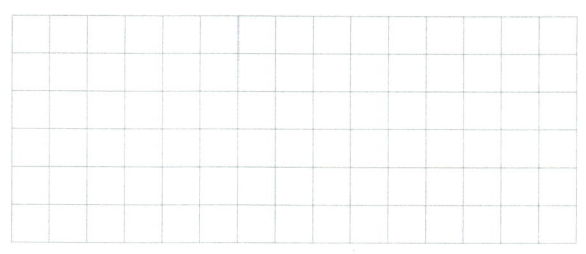

b) Explain the significance of the Hmong family for Walt's sense of belonging.

**15** Read the following characterization of Thao and correct the mistakes.

Thao Vang Lor is a teenage Hmong American. With his mother, his grandmother and his older sister Sue he lives in a house in the city centre of Detroit. He is short and of slight build. At the beginning of the film he lacks self-confidence and direction, doing the chores that his sister orders him to do such as doing the laundry and taking care of the rabbits. His cousin's gang wants to take advantage of his weakness. Initially Thao resists their offer to support and protect him, but then the gang increase their pressure, finally coercing Thao into stealing his neighbor's flag as an act of initiation. His attempt fails and as a consequence, he makes amends by doing hard physical work for his neighbor Walt. He constantly complains and shows a lack of discipline and determination, thereby earning Walt's disrespect. Over time Thao gains self-confidence and eventually musters the courage to ask Youa out for a date. In addition, Thao starts to work as a clerk in a shop and thereby develops a sense of independence. These changes can clearly be traced back to Walt's guidance and friendship.

**Part 3: Watch the movie from 1:16:45 to 1:51:50**

**16**    The following conversation takes place when Walt has locked Thao in the basement (1:36:18).

> **THAO**
> You let me out, you crazy old fuck, or I will kill you when I get out of here.
>
> *Tao pounds on the door. Walt pounds back with a strength and authority which startles Tao.*
>
> **WALT**
> You want to know how it feels to kill a man? It feels goddamned lousy. And it feels even worse when you get a medal for bravery right after you mowed down some scared kid when he tries to give up. A dumb, scared, little gook, just about your age. I shot him with the same rifle you just held upstairs.
>
> I've thought about that kid for fifty years. And I promise you, boy, you want no part of it. Me, I've got blood on my hands. I'm soiled. Forgive me for tricking you like a dope. I'll call someone and have them let you out later.
>
> **THAO**
> No! Let me out!!
>
> *Tao pounds on the door.*
>
> **WALT**
> You've come a long way. I'm proud to call you a friend. You have your whole life ahead of you, whereas this is what I do. I finish things. You'd just get in the way. Sorry.
>
> *Walt goes back upstairs, leaving Tao locked up in his cellar. Tao howls to be let out.*

Interpret the given scene with special emphasis on Walt's relationship with Thao and on the influence of Father Janovich on Walt. The following questions and phrases might be helpful.

| |
| --- |
| Why does Walt lock Thao in the basement and what does this tell us about Walt's feelings for Thao? |

| |
| --- |
| Why does Walt talk about his memories at this very moment? |

| |
| --- |
| Why does Walt talk about his memories to Thao? |

| |
| --- |
| What sort of conversation is this, what does it remind you of? |

- to develop a close relationship – *ein enges Verhältnis entwickeln*
- to feel close to somebody
- to protect someone – *jdn. schützen*
- to feel responsible for someone / to show responsibility
- to admit one's guilt – *seine Schuld zugeben*
- to confess one's sins – *seine Sünden bekennen*
- burden – *Last*
- to regret sth. – *etw. bedauern*
- to go to confession – *zur Beichte gehen*

**17**    One topic of *Gran Torino* is the different ways people deal with their sins. Provide examples from the film (write down names of characters, scenes, places etc.), then discuss with a partner which ways you think are most helpful.

**18** Read the following posts published in an internet forum. Then reply to two of them.

 I have just watched *Gran Torino* and I'm trying to make sense of my feelings towards the protagonist. I was disgusted at first, especially by his racist remarks towards his neighbors and by the way he talks to Thao, who is innocently asking for jumper cables. But I can't help finding the man somewhat likeable, even from the beginning. I'm not sure why.

*TopTom90*

 From the moment I started watching the film I felt pity for Walt. And this feeling intensified as I continued watching. He is so lonely and it seemed to me from the beginning that he is somewhat out of place, somewhat lost. But I'm not sure why, does anyone else share this feeling?

*allyh2017*

 When I first watched *Gran Torino*, I was disappointed. I had hoped for a movie which doesn't provide stereotypes. But it does: most of the women are weak characters, the hero of the movie is a white man and Thao is only happy once he is fully americanized by Walt.

*meera_k*

Reply to post by _____

Reply to post by _____

**19** Write a characterization of Walt. Take into consideration the information that you have collected about Walt in the course of this chapter.

**20** Work with a partner. Discuss whether Walt is a hero. When thinking about your answer, take into consideration the roles religion and fatherhood play.

① 

② 

We Love
We Share
We Play
We Laugh
We Fight
*Family*
We Live

③

④

"Will you still love me when I outearn you?"

## A – Fundamental Aspects

**1** a) What do the pictures tell you about families? Exchange your views with a partner. Use the terms from the box.

> extended family *(Großfamilie)* • nuclear family *(Kernfamilie)* • familial bonds • kinship *(Blutsverwandtschaft)* • to be related to one another • to rely on sb. • to be divorced • to enjoy sb.'s company • to avoid solitude *(Einsamkeit vermeiden)* • a stable/distant/close/beneficial relationship • to develop/break a bond with sb. • shared responsibilities • (step)-siblings *((Stief-)Geschwister)* • to be estranged from • material success

b) Talk about the aspects concerning families. If you had to add further aspects to the ones depicted above, what pictures would you choose?

c) Present your ideas to a partner. Decide together which of the pictures above you would replace with one of your suggestions. Give reasons.

**2**    a) Read the text, then complete the tasks on pp. 37-38.

**Family**

The Macmillan dictionary defines 'family' as "a group of people who live together and are related to one another." This rather open definition of the term already hints at the many different forms family can take in modern times. Many contemporary family scholars view 'family' as a social construct
5  and recognize the fluid, complex, and varied understandings of family. And yet the traditional so-called **nuclear family** that consists of mother, father and their children living together in the same house is still regarded as the basic social unit by many. However, gender roles within this unit have changed. Today about 72% Americans think of a marriage as ideal when husband and
10  wife both work and share child and household duties, whereas in the past the husband was the sole breadwinner. Dual incomes provide financial stability and thus basic family needs such as housing, food and healthcare as well as extracurricular expenses can be met with more easily. Some claim that nuclear families tend to be more resilient when faced with obstacles as they learn
15  to solve problems together and support each other emotionally. However, divorce and remarriage rates, which are higher in the US than anywhere else in the Western world, show that the concept of family – and therewith the idea of the nuclear family as a generally accepted ideal – has undergone significant changes. American families are more diverse than ever. As a consequence,
20  many children either grow up in **single-parent households**, where one parent, usually the mother, takes care of the children, or in blended families. Single parenthood might add pressure and stress to the job of raising children since there is no one to share day-to-day responsibilities or decision-making. Yet the number of single-parent families in the U.S. has increased significantly
25  since 1970. Apart from high divorce rates and nonmarital births, increased employment opportunities for women as well as better welfare benefits are reasons for this increase, since women are no longer dependent on a man as the breadwinner. Sometimes, however, external aspects are responsible for children growing up in single-parent households. African-American children
30  in particular suffer from living in such households as a consequence of arrest. Half of the estimated 2.3 million inmates in stately prisons are incarcerated parents with children under 18. Living in these one-parent households as a consequence of arrest might lead to economic hardship, loneliness, stigma and humiliation.

35  Many divorcees choose to get married again, so that children become part of **blended families** which involve two separate families merging into one new unit, since partners bring along their children from previous marriages or relationships. Yet, things rarely progress smoothly when families 'blend' to create stepfamilies. Children, for instance, may resist changes, since they
40  are afraid of losing a stable relationship with their natural parents. Apart from the desire to maintain relationships they do not easily form new ones and might be worried about living with new stepsiblings. In contrast, parents are likely to approach the new marriage with positive expectations and joy. As a consequence, both parents and children can become frustrated when the
45  new family doesn't function like the previous one.

Sometimes friends become part of family structures by means of '**voluntary kin**' –  that means individuals who are considered family regardless of their legal or blood connection. For example, they have a say in wills or medical directions, or take on the role of legal guardian. These self-constructed
50  families are particularly common among African-Americans and immigrant

---

**fluid** – *fließend*

**sole breadwinner** – *einziger Verdiener*

**resilient** – *widerstandsfähig*

**divorce** – *Scheidung*
→ **to divorce sb.** – *sich von jmdm. scheiden lassen*

**nonmarital** – *nicht ehelich*

**incarcerated** – *eingesperrt*

**humiliation** – *Demütigung*

**sibling** – brothers and sister

**previous** – the one before

**kin** – all the people in your family
**will** – *Testament*

communities, as well as gay and lesbian networks providing a sense of belonging. Yet, voluntary kinship might also create complications like disappointment from unfulfilled responsibility or unwanted interference.

55 While in modern Western cultures family units are usually small, in other cultures families are much larger. The so-called **extended family** includes different generations living under one roof (grandparents, parents, children, possibly even others) and sharing duties such as raising children or keeping up with household duties. Even though living together in a large family might be an economic necessity, for many it also seems to be a matter of respect 60 and mutual responsibility. In contrast to western culture, where the self is given preference over the family and where the individual decides personal matters such as marriage, eastern cultures are more family centric. Instead of individuality and independence the bond with the family has first priority and is responsible for grown-up children staying with their parents. Helping out 65 and looking after each other are certainly advantages; yet, the family always knows everyone's business, which may result in a lack of privacy.

For many Americans the ideal of the traditional family is just an idea, not reality. This ideal might best be found in immigrant families that, like Asian-American families for example, are exceptionally stable, as they are half as 70 likely to be divorced as Americans in general.

**interference** – *Einmischung*

**mutual** – *beiderseitig*

b) Note down the different family concepts that are mentioned. What are the benefits and problems of these concepts as outlined in the text? Consider the childrens' and the parents' perspectives.

| concept | benefits | problems |
|---|---|---|
| nuclear family | financial stability, more resilient | |

c) Compare your results with a partner. Can you think of more benefits/problems? Use a different color and add them to the list.

**3** Read the German expressions and find the equivalent highlighted English expressions in the text. There are more highlighted expressions in the text than necessary.

| German expression | English equivalent |
|---|---|
| *die Dinge verlaufen selten glatt* | |
| *etwas einfacher bewältigen können* | |
| *miteinander verwandt sein* | |
| *dem Ich wird Vorrang eingeräumt über* | |
| *wird immer noch gesehen als* | |
| *ein allgemein anerkanntes Ideal* | |
| *Angst haben, eine stabile Beziehung zu verlieren* | |
| *eine Ehe für ideal halten* | |

**4** a) Which of the following collocations can be used in the context of 'family life'?
Tick ☑ possible combinations and be able to explain the meaning of each collocation.

1. to share
   ☐ household duties
   ☐ all experience
   ☐ knowledge

2. to provide
   ☐ financial security
   ☐ protection
   ☐ service

3. to undergo
   ☐ significant change
   ☐ transformation
   ☐ surgery

4. economic
   ☐ hardships
   ☐ benefit
   ☐ acknowledgement

5. to maintain
   ☐ a relationship
   ☐ integrity
   ☐ weight

6. a lack of
   ☐ privacy
   ☐ support
   ☐ confidence

b) Compare your results with a partner. Agree on the most likely collocation in the context of family life.

**5** The text 'Family' on pp. 36-37 formulates some claims without giving evidence. Have a look at the following statistics. Analyze whether they support the claims made in the text.

a) Prepare a short presentation for a partner about the information provided by the following statistics. Explain whether any of the information can be used to support the claims in the text.

**Partner A:** Statistics 1 and 2 (below)    **Partner B:** Statistics 3 and 4 (on p. 40)

b) Speculate together which concepts will be more prominent/less prominent in 20 years. Give reasons.

**Statistic 1**

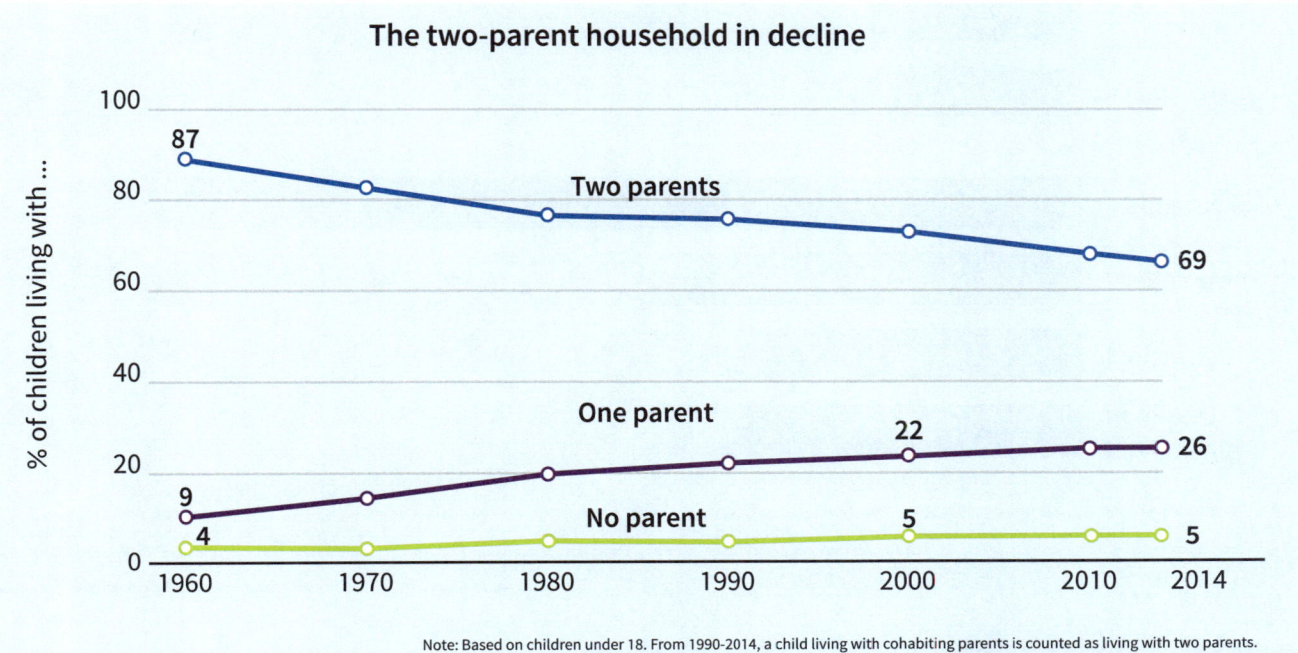

Note: Based on children under 18. From 1990-2014, a child living with cohabiting parents is counted as living with two parents. Prior to 1990 cohabiting parents are included in "one parent." Source: Pew Research Center analysis or 1960-2000 Decennial Census and 2010 and 2014 American Community Survey (IPUMS)

**Statistic 2**

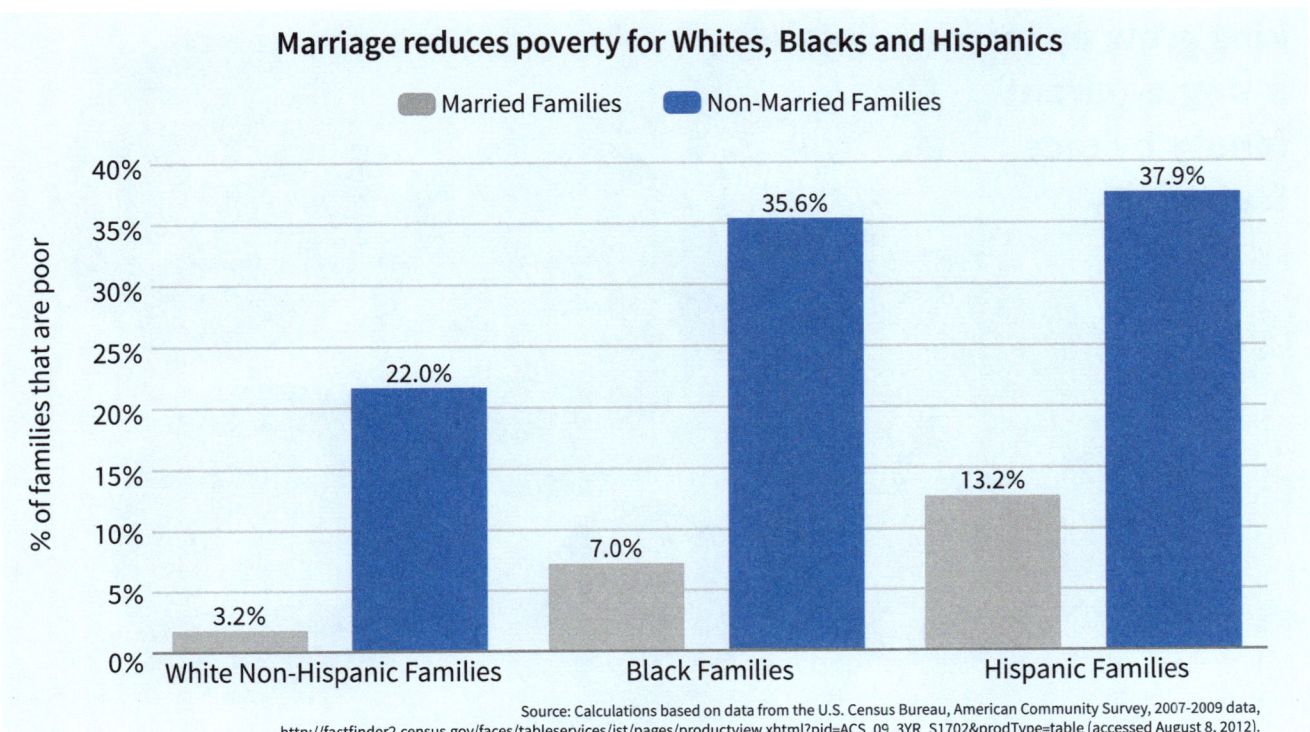

Source: Calculations based on data from the U.S. Census Bureau, American Community Survey, 2007-2009 data, http://factfinder2.census.gov/faces/tableservices/jst/pages/productview.xhtml?pid=ACS_09_3YR_S1702&prodType=table (accessed August 8, 2012).

**Statistic 3**

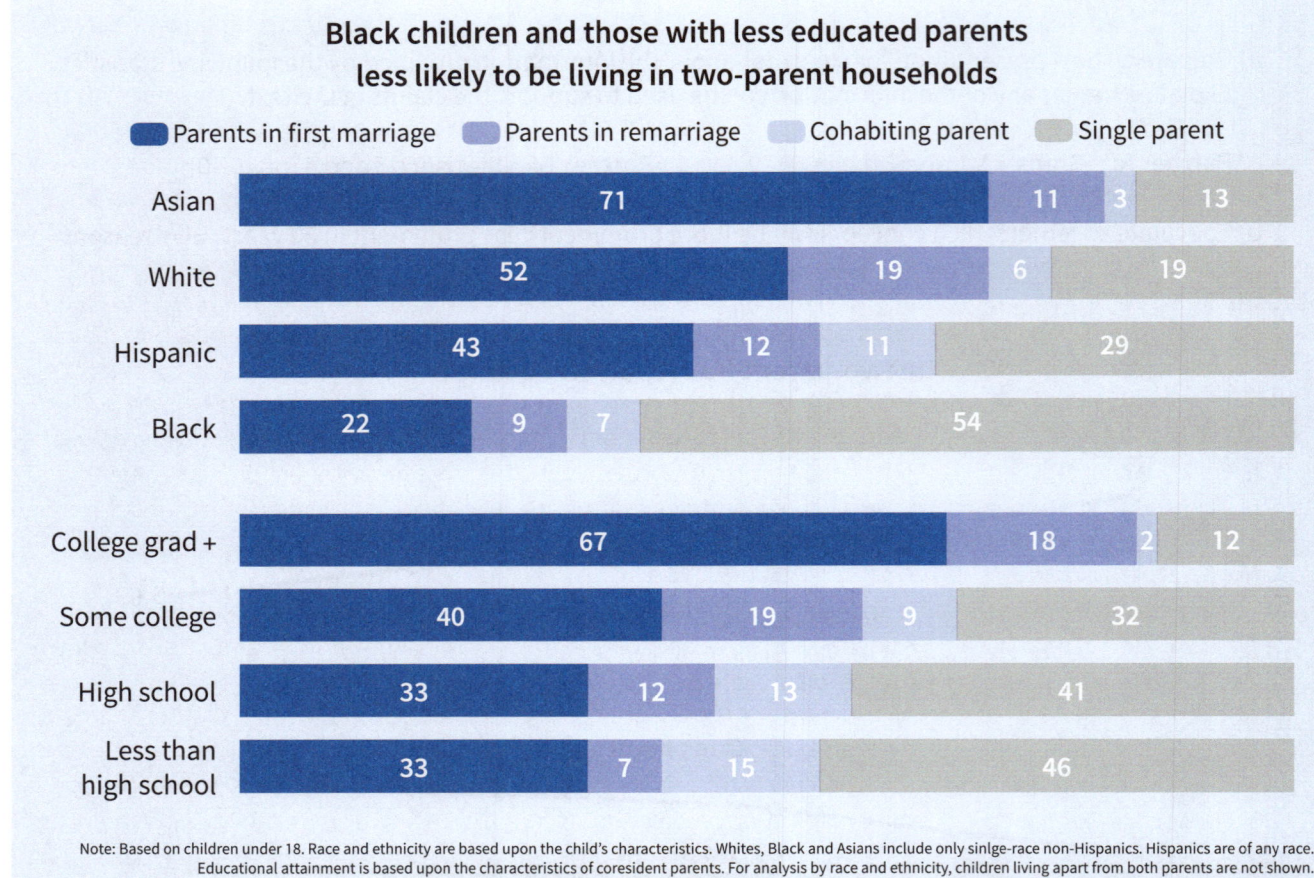

Black children and those with less educated parents less likely to be living in two-parent households

**Legend:** Parents in first marriage · Parents in remarriage · Cohabiting parent · Single parent

| | Parents in first marriage | Parents in remarriage | Cohabiting parent | Single parent |
|---|---|---|---|---|
| Asian | 71 | 11 | 3 | 13 |
| White | 52 | 19 | 6 | 19 |
| Hispanic | 43 | 12 | 11 | 29 |
| Black | 22 | 9 | 7 | 54 |
| College grad + | 67 | 18 | 2 | 12 |
| Some college | 40 | 19 | 9 | 32 |
| High school | 33 | 12 | 13 | 41 |
| Less than high school | 33 | 7 | 15 | 46 |

Note: Based on children under 18. Race and ethnicity are based upon the child's characteristics. Whites, Black and Asians include only sinlge-race non-Hispanics. Hispanics are of any race. Educational attainment is based upon the characteristics of coresident parents. For analysis by race and ethnicity, children living apart from both parents are not shown. For educational analysis, children living apart from both parents are excluded from analysis. Figures may not add to 100% due to rounding.

Source: Pew Research Center anaylsis of 2014 American Community Survey (IPUMS)

**Statistic 4**

**Likelihood that kids grow up in a single-parent family**, by race & ethnicity in 2016

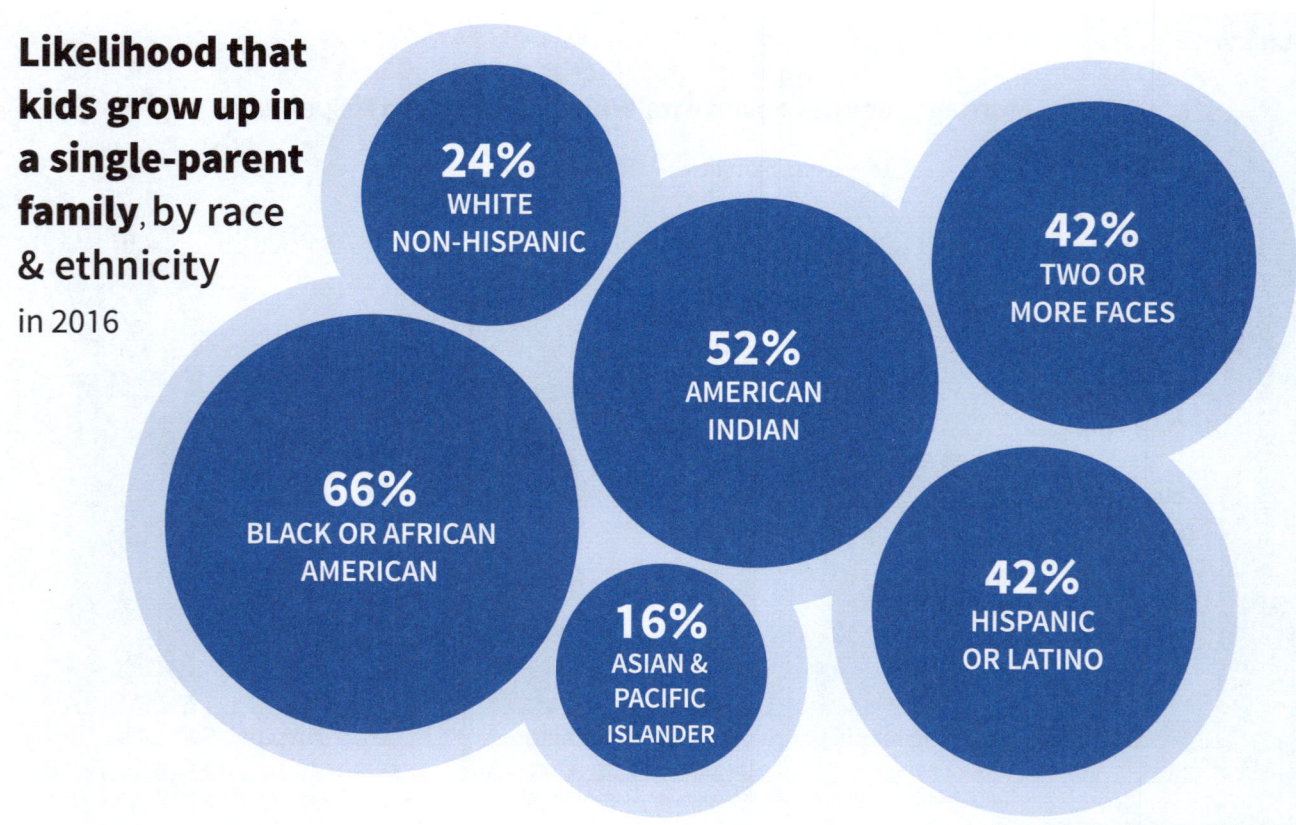

- 24% WHITE NON-HISPANIC
- 52% AMERICAN INDIAN
- 42% TWO OR MORE FACES
- 66% BLACK OR AFRICAN AMERICAN
- 16% ASIAN & PACIFIC ISLANDER
- 42% HISPANIC OR LATINO

Source: The Annie E. Casey Foundation, 2018

# B – Focus on belonging

to rely on sb. • to trust sb. • mutual trust *(gegenseitiges Vertrauen)* • trustworthy • to care about sb. •
loyalty • to stay loyal to sb. • to stay by sb.'s side • to get on well with sb. • to care about sb. •
to be fond of sb. *(jmd. mögen)* • to share secrets with sb. • make friends with sb. • to enjoy being with sb. •
to lose touch with • to protect sb. from • to rely on sb. • to feel safe/appreciated/welcome/secure •
a best/close/closest/dear/lifelong/trusted friend • to have a lot in common

**1**  Think about the following questions and then talk to a partner about them. The words in the box might help you.

a) Discuss why people make friends. Include the theories from p. 6.

b) What does a friend have to be like in order to be a *real* friend?

c) Discuss the following quote: *"I will immediately end a friendship if I am lied to."*

d) Think of situations where you would end a friendship.

**2**  a) From a scale of 1 (not important at all) to 10 (very important), rank the importance of a) family and b) friends in your life today (red), ten years ago (blue) and in twenty years (green). Give reasons.

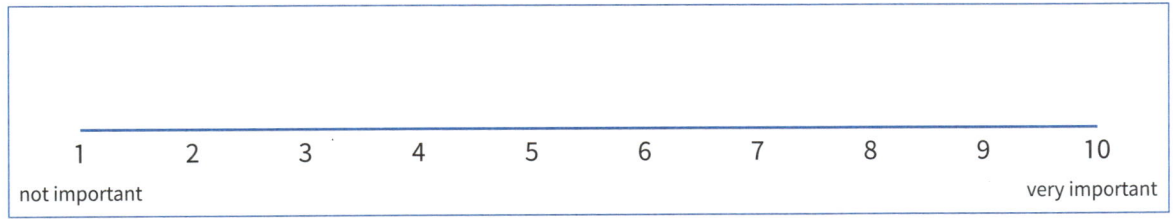

| 1 | 2 | 3 | 4 | 5 | 6 | 7 | 8 | 9 | 10 |
|---|---|---|---|---|---|---|---|---|---|
| not important | | | | | | | | | very important |

b) Exchange your results with a partner.

**3**  *"In Western societies, it is no longer the family that provides a sense of belonging, but rather friends and colleagues."*

a) Think about the quote for a minute. Do you agree or disagree with the position given in the quote? Exchange your views with a partner.

b) Skim the two comments on pp. 42-43. Do they agree or disagree with the quote? You only have 30 seconds to find out. At first sight: Which one do you like better? Why?

c) Read the comments again and label each paragraph using the words from the box.
Add a description of the purpose it serves. Use the space on the right-hand side.

conclusion • main part • introduction • argument 1 • example 1 • argument 2 • ...

**Comment 1**

Our world has changed significantly over the past 20 years, and these changes have affected all areas of life. People have never had so many opportunities to meet and communicate with other people, thanks to the countless new forms of digital communication. These have radically altered both our personal lives and our work lives. Personal relationships are essential for human beings because they quench our thirst for belonging. There are some who argue that the modern individual no longer draws his or her sense of belonging from the family, but rather feels a greater emotional attachment to work colleagues and friends. In the following brief essay, I'd like to comment on this claim.

There is no doubt that colleagues and friends provide us with some sense of belonging. Many people are on good terms with their colleagues and consider their place of work a "home from home". Yet in the recent past, working conditions have changed substantially, with employers demanding an increased degree of flexibility from their staff. As a consequence, many people move from one project or job to the next, without ever really settling down and establishing stable relationships within the workplace. Friendships are also affected adversely by the great flexibility required of the modern worker. The number of people who have to move because of their jobs is constantly growing. In these circumstances, it can be extremely difficult to maintain friendships. There are, of course, people who maintain life-long friendships, but they are the exceptions. Most friendships only work if people meet up in person on a regular basis, and relations often start to cool when friends stop taking the time to see one another.

While our personal lives can sometimes feel like a revolving door of new friends and acquaintances, family life remains a constant. Relationships within the family are far less susceptible to change. The nuclear family, which consists of children and their parents, – mother, father and children, in some cases mother, mother and children or father, father and children – usually sticks together. People spend a great proportion of their lives nestled in the security of this social unit. By this I don't literally mean that every family gathers around the TV set every night, or sits down most evenings to play a board game together. The need for belonging can also be satisfied simply by knowing that your family is around. Then there is the extended family, who usually get together on occasions such as birthdays, baptisms and weddings, even if the various family members live at a great distance from each other.

So why is it that familial bonds are the hardest to be broken? Friendships usually have to be mutually beneficial in some way, and if one of a pair of friends begins to tire of the other, then the friendship is not likely to last. In families, however, people are connected by ties that transcend the appeal of personality. In particular the relationship between parents and children is marked by unconditional love and acceptance. Thus, both parents and children can foster a sense of belonging without feeling any pressure or fear. This phenomenon has its roots in biology. One generation prepares the way for the next. By providing a home in which their children can flourish, parents simultaneously discover their own sense of belonging within the natural order.

One may argue that in the past fifty years we have witnessed a decline in traditional family structures. Divorce rates have increased, and there are more and more single parent households. And it is certainly true that it is more difficult for divorced parents to convince their children of the security and comfort that can be found in a family. But the simple fact that children suffer so much from divorces is evidence that families are more important than colleagues and friends when it comes to providing a sense of belonging. Friends and colleagues may play important roles during times of crisis, but they can never replace the family.

*introduction – the author explains the meaning of the quote to the reader and ...*

**Comment 2**

Having a sense of belonging in one's life is an innate human need. Belonging can be defined as the emotional desire to be an accepted member of a certain group. Seeking connectedness with others seems to contribute a greater meaning to life for the individual as it makes us feel wanted and needed. It therefore goes without saying that human life is greatly affected by this drive. "Do I fit in?" is a question especially young people often ask themselves. Some people find belonging with family, others with friends. Some only need one or two people to connect with, others need more. For many, family is the key to developing a strong sense of belonging. However, for me as a teenager, it is friends who influence my sense of belonging the most. In the following essay I intend to present arguments in favor of my position.

Many people argue that family is the most important factor to foster a strong sense of belonging. It is the family you are born into, the first people you communicate with, the place, they claim, where your values, norms, rituals and traditions are moulded from the very beginning. However, developing a sense of belonging is a continuous process and there are times in life where friends are closer to you than your family. For me as a teenager, it is especially difficult to find a sense of belonging in the traditions, values and norms that my parents stand for. People always say that puberty is a difficult time for a teenager, since one has to find one's way in life aside from what adults seem to find important. In this phase of transition friends are closer in terms of age, morals, beliefs and life style. Whereas I feel completely misunderstood at home, my friends share my problems and experiences and I feel understood and accepted. Simply put, it is not family where I find belongingness right now – it is my friends instead.

On top of that, family structures and the idea of family as the guarantor of belongingness have changed over the last 50 years. In modern times society is confronted with a decline of the traditional paradigm family. Divorce rates, for example, have increased significantly over the last 50 years as well as the number of single parent households. As a consequence, the relationship between parents, children and other family members has undergone a substantial change. Many of my friends have to cope with estranged parents. Finding a sense of belonging is not easy when your father and mother are in constant conflict, when only one of them is there for you at a certain time. That's why friends have become more important when it comes to belongingness for many of my peers.

Last but not least, friends are people you have established relationships with without being inevitably related to them. And last of all, as the saying goes: "You can choose your friends, but you can't choose your family." What it means is that you can't do anything about kinship. Your friend is who you choose on the basis of shared beliefs, same interests, same lifestyle … . I don't have much in common with my brother and we rarely talk. Even though I feel connected to him, since he is my brother, my best friend is the one who provides support and the feeling of acceptance. I feel understood and he does too. The close bonds that we have both chosen deliberately are an invaluable means of finding my sense of belonging in life and provide me with the necessary support to confront challenges.

Friends or family – the conclusion I draw is as follows: although I can understand that family is the key to developing a sense of belonging for many, from my point of view there are phases in life where your friends are more important in that respect. In the period between teenage life and adolescence, friends, for me, are crucial, especially since traditional family concepts have increasingly lost their potential to offer a reliable and safe haven at this formative time in a young person's life.

**4** a) Have a look at the structure of the two comments.

- Analyze whether introductions and conclusions are included.
- Summarize the key arguments in the boxes below. Rate them from very strong (++) to very weak (--).
- Summarize the given examples. Rate them from very strong (++) to very weak (--).

| Comment A | |
|---|---|
| Argument | Example |
| | |

| Comment B | |
|---|---|
| Argument | Example |
| | |

b) Compare and assess the two comments, not based on the opinion that is given, but on the quality of the comment (structure, content, use of language).

| Assessment | |
|---|---|
| | |

**5** A comment is characterized by a clear structure. In order to help the reader understand your line of argumentation, it is a good idea to use 'signposts' that immediately show the reader whether to expect, for instance, a fact, a speculation, a contradiction or a consequence.

a) Have a look at the phrases in the box below and put them into the categories on the next page. Once you are done, add examples of your own.

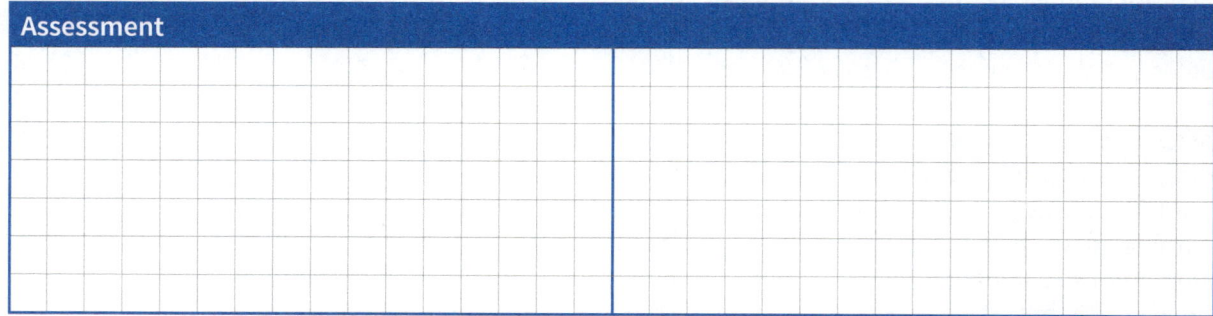

one could argue that ... • personally, I believe that ... • it seems highly likely that ... • to sum up, ... • there is no proof/evidence that ... • there is no doubt that ... • however, ... • as/since ... • given that ... • unlike the author/cartoonist, I think that ... • consequently, ... • in comparison with ... • to sum up, ... • for this reason, ... • such as ... • in short ... • another aspect that needs to be considered is ...

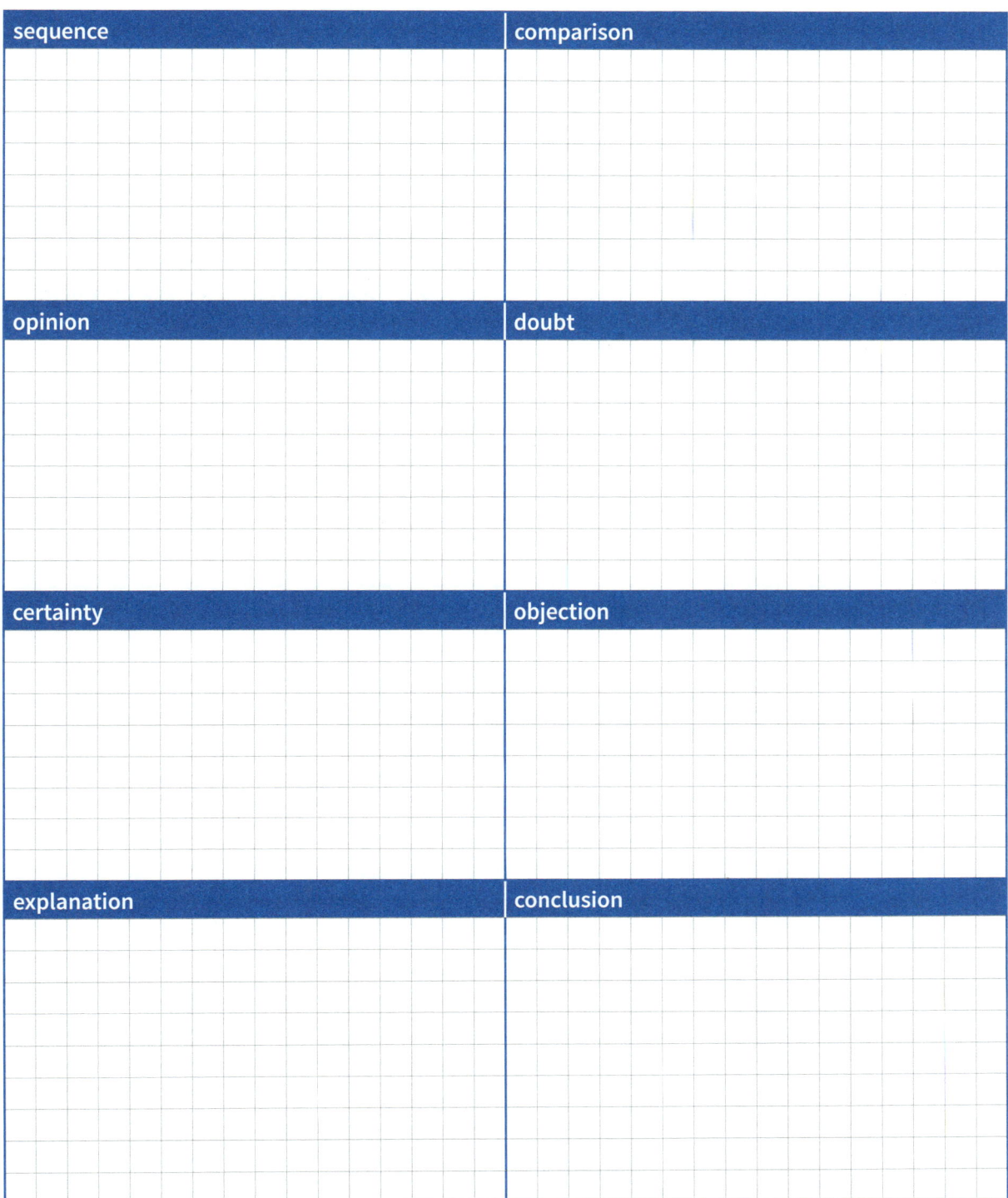

| sequence | comparison |
|---|---|
| | |

| opinion | doubt |
|---|---|
| | |

| certainty | objection |
|---|---|
| | |

| explanation | conclusion |
|---|---|
| | |

**6**  Comment on one of the following quotes.

"Belonging to one group pushes us away from another group."

"Our identity is shaped by our relationships."

Before you start writing, make notes on any terms you want to use in your introduction, main part and conclusion. Look at your notes from B3c) for help.

📖 **How to write a comment → see skills pp. 102-103**

**7**  Exchange your text with a partner and give feedback. To do so, highlight the arguments and the supporting examples in one color and the signposts in another. Assess whether they show where your partner is heading.

## C – Focus on film and short story

**1**   In A2b) (p. 37) you listed different family concepts and their possible advantages as well as disadvantages.

a) Find examples of those concepts in *The child* and *Gran Torino*.
   Note down problems and benefits for both.

| concepts | examples from *The child* / *Gran Torino* | benefits | problems |
|---|---|---|---|
| nuclear family | • Walt´s family | • children looking after their father | • lack of real interest |
| single-parent-household | | | |
| extended family | | | |
| voluntary kinship | | | |

b) Compare your results with those in A2b). Talk to a partner about your findings. What do they tell you about the importance of family in the short story and the film?

**2** The following graph is meant to visualize the degree of closeness/distance between Walt and the other main characters. The x-axis stands for Walt's life, the y-axis shows the degree of closeness/distance to the other characters.

a) Fill out the following graph for Walt and the central characters (Thao, Father Janovich, Mitch and Sue).

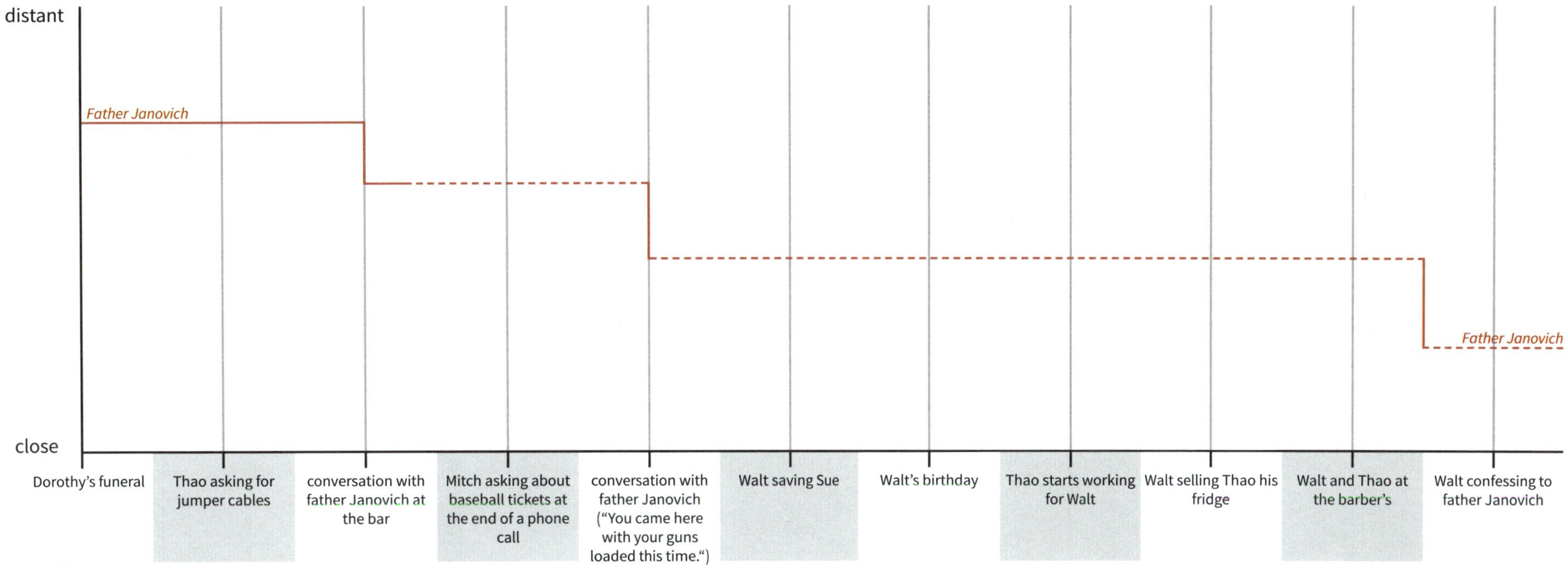

b) Present and explain your results. Take notes.

**3** a) In 1914 Egon Schiele painted this portrait of Heinrich Bensch and his son Otto. Circle the important elements in the picture and describe them.

📖 **How to analyze and interpret pictures p. 104**

> a failed/strained *(angespannt)*/troubled/superficial relationship • distant/close • to be clearly superior to *(überlegen)* • to withdraw from • to distance oneself from • to keep one's distance • to put pressure on • to order sb. about • to humiliate sb. *(demütigen)* • to adopt the father role for sb. • to offer sb. safety • to feel alienated from sb. *(entfremdet)* • to feel kinship with sb. • to feel closely connected to • to be possessive/bossy/dominant ↔ to be submissive/obedient *(unterwürfig)* • to keep sb. at a distance • to develop a bond with sb. • to feel loyalty towards sb.

b) Using the words from the box above, assess the father-son relationship shown here.

c) Assess whether the painting could be used to illustrate the father-son-relationships in the film. Give reasons for your opinion.

**4** Who do the following characters from the short story and the film turn to in order to feel a sense of belonging?

| character | options |
|-----------|---------|
| Karen | |
| Walt | |
| Thao | |

**5** Choose one of the following tasks:

a) "Blood is thicker than water." Imagine you are Thao or Walt. Comment on the quote.

b) Both Walt and Karen are lonely. Comment on the statement.

## A – Fundamental aspects

**1**  a) Put the pictures into chronological order. Give reasons for your decisions.

oldest ⟶ most recent

picture _____    picture _____    picture _____    picture _____    picture _____

b) Describe the idea of the American Dream as depicted in the pictures above. Use the words from the box.

> economic security · freedom · happiness · wealth · equal opportunity · democracy ·
> sense of belonging · discrimination · fair treatment · independence · prosperity *(Wohlstand)* ·
> religious persecution *(Verfolgung aus religiösen Gründen)* · poverty · exclusion · material success ·
> to gain · to reach out for · to seek · to strive for · to escape from · to suffer from · to fear ·
> to avoid · to get rid of

c) Put yourself in the position of one of the circled people. Take notes on the following question from their point of view: **What does the American Dream mean to me?** Include words from the box.

d) Exchange your ideas with a classmate who chose a different person. Talk about similarities and differences.

e) What about you? Rank the ideas of the American Dream as mentioned above according to their significance for you.

**Info box**

**The American Dream**

In 1931, in the midst of the Great Depression, James Truslow Adams, an American historian, published a book called *The Epic of America*, in which he dealt with what he described as the "American Dream". The concept itself had existed long before Adams and stood in stark contrast to the European concept of social hierarchy at that time *(Ständegesellschaft)*. As early as 1630, John Winthrop envisioned his idea of a "city upon the hill", a city in which everybody had the chance to prosper and succeed in life, in a sermon to his fellow Puritan colonists. And in 1776, The Declaration of Independence emphasized the idea of everybody being entitled to "life, liberty and pursuit of happiness". Since 1931 the term has become a catchphrase for the lure and the promise of the new continent – whether it is real or simply a myth.

**2**  a) Read the following extracts, which all illustrate the American Dream, then do the tasks on the next page.

If […] the things already listed were all we had had to contribute, America would have made no distinctive and unique gift to mankind. But there has been also the American dream, the dream of a land in which life should be better and richer and fuller for every man, with opportunity for each according to his ability or achievement. It is a difficult dream for the European upper classes to interpret
5  adequately, and too many of us ourselves have grown weary and mistrustful of it. It is not a dream of motor cars and high wages merely, but a dream of a social order in which each man and each woman shall be able to attain to the fullest stature of which they are innately capable, and be recognized by others for what they are, regardless of the fortuitous circumstances of birth or position.
*(James Truslow Adams, The Epic of America, New York: Blue Ribbon Books, 1931)*

As the child of immigrant parents, I grew up knowing education was important. Ever since I could
10  remember, my parents told me I was going to college. My mom was able to finish her high-school education, but my dad barely made it to the third grade. Their lack of higher education made them adamant of emphasizing to me and my siblings the importance of attending school.
When people talk about the American Dream they share stories about people who "started at the bottom and made it to the top", people who had no money and later made a fortune by using their
15  street smarts or inventions. […] The dream for today is being free from mass terror and being able to have simple human rights: water, a home, education, faith, and simply being able to walk down the street without thinking if the person next to you is carrying a gun that can kill you in seconds.
*(https://www.theodysseyonline.com/reinventing-the-american-dream)*

"[…] I grew up poor in the Rust Belt, in an Ohio steel town […]. My grandparents, neither of whom graduated from high school, raised me, and few members of even my extended family attended
20  college. The statistics tell you that kids like me face a grim future  –  that if they're lucky, they'll manage to avoid welfare, and if they're unlucky, they'll die of a heroin overdose, as happened to dozens in my small hometown just last year. I was one of those kids with a grim future. I almost failed out of high school. I nearly gave in to the deep anger and resentment harbored by everyone around me. Today people look at me, at my job and my Ivy League credentials, and assume that I'm some sort of genius,
25  that only a truly extraordinary person could have made it to where I am today. With all due respect to those people, I think that theory is a load of bullshit. Whatever talents I have, I almost squandered until a handful of loving people rescued me."
*(J. D. Vance, Hillbilly Elegy, New York: Harper, 2016, pp. 1-2)*

"To get out beyond successful neighborhoods in DC, New York City and the elite college campuses … is to see another America. […] It is an America that has been on a downward trajectory for decades, hurt
30  by the loss of jobs and with downtowns emptied of energy and filled with drugs. It has made staying in these communities harder. In this America hope is fading, not growing. People's lives are a constant tangle of changing and uncertain jobs. The path that offers a way out – education – requires threading a narrow needle of opportunities from an early age. If that small chance is missed it means a lifetime of feeling looked down on by the "other America."
*(https://www.theguardian.com/society/2017/feb/21/outside-coastal-bubbles-to-say-america-is-already-great-rings-hollow)*

b) The following expressions have been taken from the texts on the previous page. Choose the German translation which fits best in the given context.

| English term | German equivalent |
|---|---|
| … with opportunity for each (l. 3) | ☐ Möglichkeiten/Chancen<br>☐ Regeln<br>☐ Macht |
| …according to his ability or achievement (ll. 3-4) | ☐ gemäß seiner Fähigkeiten oder seines Könnens<br>☐ gemäß seiner Herkunft oder seines Vermögens<br>☐ gemäß seiner Fähigkeiten oder Leistungen |
| … of which they are innately capable … (l. 7) | ☐ hat es kaum geschafft<br>☐ hat es knapp geschafft<br>☐ hat es ohne Unterstützung geschafft |
| … to barely make it (l. 11) | ☐ einer unsicheren Zukunft entgegenblicken<br>☐ eine rosige Zukunft vor sich haben<br>☐ eine düstere Zukunft bevorsteht |
| … face a grim future (l. 20) | ☐ einer unsicheren Zukunft entgegenblicken<br>☐ eine rosige Zukunft vor sich haben<br>☐ eine düstere Zukunft bevorsteht |
| … gave in to the deep anger and resentment … (l. 23) | ☐ gaben sich einer tiefgehenden Wut und Missgunst hin<br>☐ verbreiteten eine tiefgehende Wut und Missgunst<br>☐ bekämpften die tiefgehende Wut und Missgunst |
| … hope is fading, … (l. 31) | ☐ die Hoffnung schwindet<br>☐ die Hoffnung überwiegt<br>☐ die Hoffnung bleibt |
| … threading a narrow needle of opportunities … (l. 32-33) | ☐ den Faden durch eine schmale Nadel der Möglichkeiten fädeln<br>☐ einen dicken Teppich an Möglichkeiten weben<br>☐ zahlreiche Möglichkeiten in Erwägung ziehen |

c) Have a look at the pictures on p. 49 and the quotes on p. 50 again. Identify the ideas of the American Dream as presented in some of the pictures and some of the quotes. Compare them with the presentation of real life in the other pictures and quotes and draw a conclusion.

| ideas of the American Dream | real life |
|---|---|
| prosperity | |

conclusion:

**3** In order to guide the reading process and to structure an argumentative text effectively, many writers use so-called **signposts**. The following text is an argumentative essay dealing with the claim that education is important for success. The signposts still have to be added.

a) Have a look at the signpost expressions below and group them into categories (e.g. *sequencing*, *contrast* …).

> therefore • it is for this reason that • there is some evidence to suggest • some people might argue • for instance • however • a further point to consider is that • consequently • hence *(daher, deshalb)* • what also makes me doubt that the given claim is right • despite this • such as • secondly • yet • this is clearly an argument in favor of the claim • this might be an argument against the claim • having looked at the different aspects of the issue, my conclusion is

b) Using the signposts, fill in the gaps. Be careful – there are more options than needed.

c) Write the function of each signpost on the right of the model text. In a different color, note down the function of the paragraphs.

*According to the American Dream, education is important for success.*
*Does this apply in Germany as well? Discuss.*

The American Dream is the dream of a "better, richer and fuller" life. It is the dream that the next generation will be better off than the previous one. It is also the dream that these goals can be achieved through hard work – by everyone, regardless of their background. According to modern versions of the dream, it is not physical labour which leads to success, but working hard towards getting a good education.

*introduction*

In the following text, I will discuss whether education is crucial for success in Germany, providing arguments and examples both in favor of and against this claim. When I use the word "success" in this essay, I mean financial success. When I use the word "education", I am referring to university degrees, not to basic education.

*announcing the plan*
*definition of key term*

My parents, my teachers, my friends and my relatives all tell me that I need to work hard at school in order to achieve good grades and get a degree, because this is the key to success. Indeed, for many well-paid jobs – __**for instance, such as**__ engineers, doctors, lawyers, bank managers or architects – you need university degrees and the better your grades, the more likely you will be employed. __**This is clearly an argument in favor of the claim**__ that education is crucial to success.

*exemplification*

*backs up the thesis and summarizes the paragraph*

_____ good education not only gets you a good job, my parents argue. Education also gives you knowledge of the world around you. It helps you to build opinions and develop a point of view. Many attractive jobs require the competence of opinion making. If you, _____ , want to work in a responsible position, you need to be able to decide on the basis for own knowledge. _____ , education is regarded as important by many.

_____ / _____ , I know many people who studied for years and gained university degrees, yet don't have well-paid jobs. Some of them even have to pay back student loans because their parents couldn't afford to pay for their living while they went to university. If they had done an apprenticeship and had started to work at an early age, they would now have earned a lot of money already. Some people who are at the same age with a university degree might never catch up. _____ , a good and comprehensive education doesn't necessarily lead to a good salary.

_____

is that in many well-paid jobs it is not your education which decides about your success. It's your willingness to take risks, your courage, your talent, your ability to communicate and often simply luck which contribute to your success. Restaurant owners, shop owners, fitness coaches and many other entrepreneurs serve as examples. They all need certain skills and experience in their jobs, yet these skills are not taught at school or at university. Education in these jobs is not important for success.

_____

that education is only important for success in some areas. For many jobs, a university degree is not necessary and success depends on factors other than education.

**4** Partners A and B: **Monologue** – Describe your image and interpret it with reference to the American Dream.

*Title: American Dream Helper; Published: Marin Independent Journal; Date: November, 2001; Artist: Steve Greenberg*

↑ **Partner B:** The cartoon was published in 2001. Compare its main message with James Truslow Adams' concept layed out in *The Epic of America*.

↑ **Partner A:** The poster refers to the 1950s. Explain what changes you would make to it (e.g. the setting and/or the people who are depicted, rewriting the text) so that it portrays the American Dream of today.

**5** Partners A and B: **Dialogue** – Discuss whether the American Dream is still alive today.

**6** a) Explain and interpret the statistic below with reference to the American Dream.

b) Compare the statistic to the following quote:

> "Our problems are man-made – therefore, they can be solved by man.
> And man can be as big as he wants. No problem of human destiny is beyond human beings."
> *(President John Kennedy's American University Commencement Speech, June 10, 1963)*

c) Discuss one of the following statements in an argumentative essay. Take into consideration what you have learned about the American Dream. The statistic below also contains information that you can include in your essay.

| You can start at the bottom and make it to the top. | The sacrifices and sweat of today will lead to a better life in the future. |

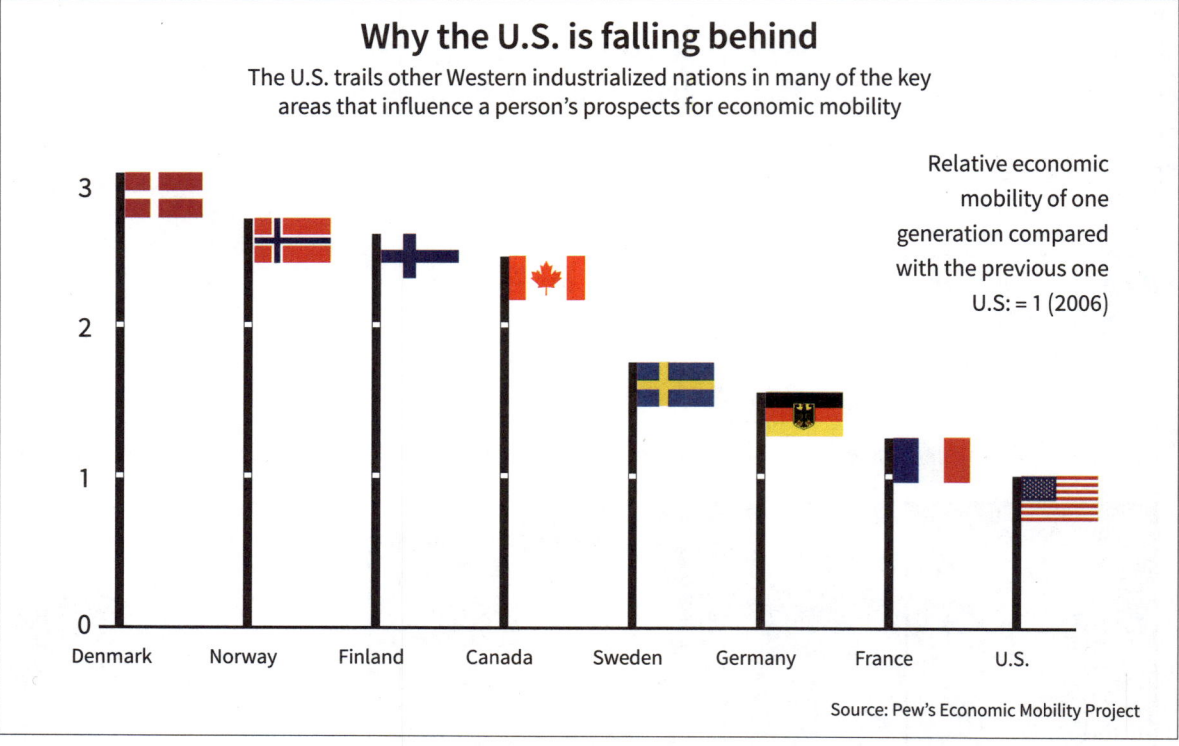

**Why the U.S. is falling behind**

The U.S. trails other Western industrialized nations in many of the key areas that influence a person's prospects for economic mobility

Relative economic mobility of one generation compared with the previous one U.S: = 1 (2006)

Denmark  Norway  Finland  Canada  Sweden  Germany  France  U.S.

Source: Pew's Economic Mobility Project

Before you start writing, take notes. Keep in mind that there are two ways to organize your arguments. Check pp. 106-107 (Skills) to decide which one you prefer.

📖 **Argumentative Essay → see skills pp. 106-107**

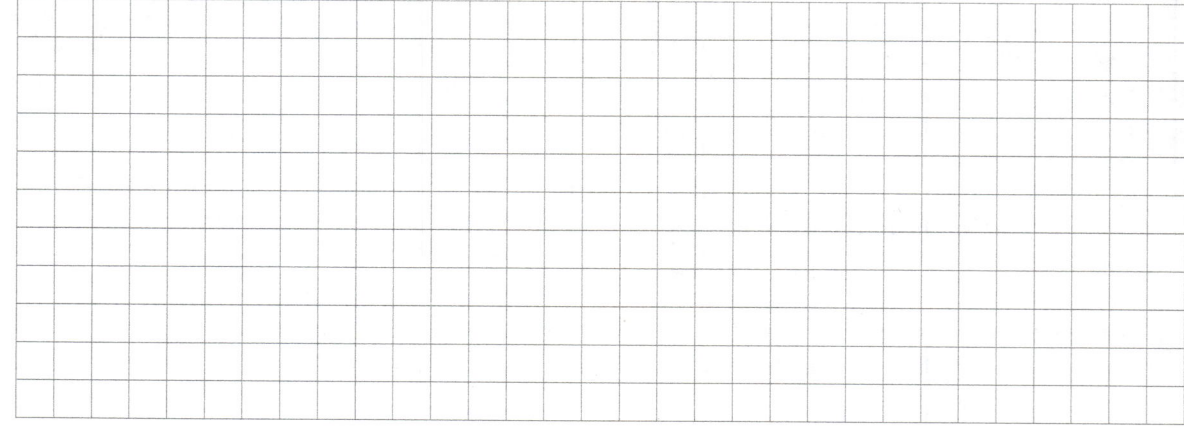

# B – Focus on belonging

**1** a) Read the following excerpt, which is taken from a speech by Barack Obama during his first election campaign in 2007. Then do the tasks on the next page.

"It's wonderful to be here today. I feel right at home in Bettendorf, which is just a stone's throw from my home state of Illinois. But the truth is, we share more than the banks of a great river.

If you spend time in Washington, you hear a lot about the divisions in our
5 country. About how we're becoming more separated by geography and ideology; race and religion; wealth and opportunity. And we've had plenty of politicians who try to take advantage of these divisions – pitting Americans against one another, or targeting different messages to different audiences.

But as I've traveled around Iowa and the rest of the country these last nine
10 months, I haven't been struck by our differences – I've been impressed by the values and hopes that we share. In big cities and small towns; among men and women; young and old; black, white, and brown – Americans share a faith in simple dreams. A job with wages that can support a family. Health care that we can count on and afford. A retirement that is dignified and secure.
15 Education and opportunity for our kids. Common hopes. American dreams. [...]

What is unique about America is that we want these dreams for more than ourselves – we want them for each other. That's why we call it the American dream. We want it for the kid who doesn't go to college because she cannot
20 afford it; for the worker who is wondering if his wages will pay this winter's heating bill; for 47 million Americans living without health care; for the millions more who worry if they have enough to retire with the dignity they have earned.

When our fellow Americans are denied the American dream, our own dreams
25 are diminished. And today, the cost of that dream is rising faster than ever before. While some have prospered beyond imagination in this global economy, middle class Americans – as well as those working hard to become middle class – are seeing the American dream slip further and further away.

You know it from your own lives. Americans are working harder for less and
30 paying more for health care and college. For most folks, one income isn't enough to raise a family and send your kids to college. Sometimes, two incomes aren't enough. It's harder to save. It's harder to retire. You're doing your part, you're meeting your responsibilities, but it always seems like you're treading water or falling behind. And as I see this every day on the campaign
35 trail, I'm reminded of how unlikely it is that the dreams of my family could be realized today.

I don't accept this future. We need to reclaim the American dream. [...] We're not going to reclaim that dream unless we put an end to the politics of polarization and division that is holding this country back; unless we stand up
40 to the corporate lobbyists that have stood in the way of progress; unless we have leadership that doesn't just tell people what they want to hear – but tells everyone what they need to know. That's the change we need.
I believe that Americans want to come together again behind a common purpose. Americans want to reclaim our American dream."

(November 7, 2007, Bettendorf, Iowa)

**division** – *Teilung, Kluft*

**to share a faith** – *an etwas gemeinsam glauben*
**retirement** – *Ruhestand*
**dignified** – *würdevoll*

**to diminish** – *schmälern*
**to prosper** – *florieren, erfolgreich sein*

**to tread water** – *auf der Stelle treten, in einer Sackgasse stecken*

**to reclaim** – *zurückfordern*

**corporate lobbyist** – *Interessensvertreter großer Unternehmen*

b) Use the tag cloud below to summarize the speech.

**2** a) According to Obama, Americans share a national identity. They feel they belong to their country. How does he define this identity, this sense of belonging? Explain.

b) Explain why Obama focuses on the **idea** of the American Dream in his speech.

**3** According to Barack Obama, Americans share common hopes and simple dreams. For him, this is what keeps the country together. Do Germans share anything that creates a national identity? Note down possible examples. Compare your results with a partner and discuss your ideas.

# C – Focus on film and short story

**1** Decide for each character listed below whether they share what Obama describes as "common hopes" and "simple dreams" in his speech. Tick ☑ and explain.

| name of character | common hopes simple dreams | explanation |
|---|---|---|
| Walt | ☐ share<br>☐ not share<br>☐ ambivalent | |
| Thao | ☐ share<br>☐ not share<br>☐ ambivalent | |
| the gang | ☐ share<br>☐ not share<br>☐ ambivalent | |
| Sue | ☐ share<br>☐ not share<br>☐ ambivalent | |
| Mitch | ☐ share<br>☐ not share<br>☐ ambivalent | |
| Karen | ☐ share<br>☐ not share<br>☐ ambivalent | |
| Karen's mother | ☐ share<br>☐ not share<br>☐ ambivalent | |

**2** Read the following passage from *The child*, and the conversation between Walt and Thao and look at the highlighted phrases. For each phrase decide which of the following aspects of the American Dream/ American life describes it best.

- the idea of a good society
- religous freedom
- equal chances and opportunities
- idea of a new beginning

- fading hope
- unlimited opportunities
- the American Dream as a nightmare

- luck
- economic prosperity
- the right to live according to your own convictions and abilities

None of that mattered now. It would be a while before she read another schoolbook, what with the baby due in March. She wanted to believe she would go back and finish after the baby came, but none of her friends who'd had babies had done that. But that was okay. Seventeen years from next spring, her baby would finish school for both of them.

Her child wasn't going to have nothing to do with winos and junkies and dirty streets and loud music. It would stay inside and read big books and be real smart, and when it got grown, it would say, "Mama, let's go. I'm going to move you out of here. I'm going to take you away from all these drunk people and junkies."

*In the following extract from "Gran Torino", Thao is talking with Walt while working in Walt's garden. (1:08:30 – 1:09:56)*

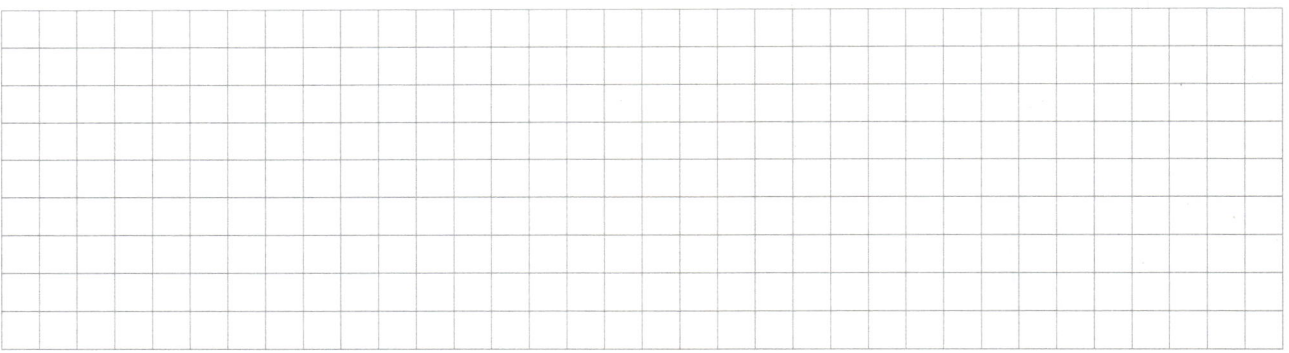

**WALT**
So, what do you want to do with your life, kid?
**THAO**
Well, I was thinking about maybe sales.
**WALT**
Sales, huh? My oldest son is in sales.
**THAO**
Does he do well?
**WALT**
Oh, yeah. License to steal. I worked in a Ford factory for fifty years and he's out selling Japanese cars.
**THAO**
You made cars?
**WALT**
Yeah. I put the steering column in this Gran Torino in 1972, right on the line.
**THAO**
Oh, you are old. So cool.

**WALT**
Yeah, so you wanna be in sales. You thinking about going to school maybe?
**THAO**
Kind of, but school costs money.
**WALT**
Well, maybe you should get a job, you can't just sit there and spread mulch in my garden the rest of your life.
**THAO**
Well, maybe you could just pay me.
**WALT**
Yeah, very funny.
**THAO**
What kind of job could I ever get?
**WALT**
Yeah, you're right, noboby would ever hire you.
**THAO**
Yeah, I know.

**WALT**
Look, I'm just kidding, zip. I mean you could get a job. You could get a job anywhere.
**THAO**
Like what?
**WALT**
Well, how about construction.
**THAO**
Me? Construction? What, do you have Alzheimer's or something?
**WALT**
No, you could get a job in construction. I know people in the trades. Course I have to make a little adjustment, man you up a little bit.
**THAO**
Man me up?
**WALT**
Yeah.

## 3 Choose

James Truslow Adams says: *"It is not a dream of motor cars and high wages merely, but a dream of a social order in which each man and each woman shall be able to attain to the fullest stature of which they are innately capable, and be recognized by others for what they are, regardless of the fortuitous circumstances of birth or position."* (James Truslow Adams, *The Epic of America*, New York: Blue Ribbon Books, 1931)

Is this dream attainable for Thao? Write an argumentative essay taking into considersation what you have learned in this chapter. Use the space below and the table on the next page to plan your essay.

**OR**

Discuss whether this dream is attainable for Karen from the short story *The child*.

Introduction

Argument 1

Example

Argument 2

Example

Argument 3

Example

Argument 4

Example

Conclusion

## A – Fundamental aspects

**1** Which aspects of immigration are portrayed in the pictures above? Talk to a partner using the words in the box.

> country of origin • homeland • destination • persecution *(Verfolgung)* • to flee a country •
> (illegal) immigrant/to immigrate to/influx of immigration *(Einwandererstrom)*/first generation immigrant •
> refugee *(Flüchtling)*/to seek refuge from • asylum seeker *(Asylbewerber)*/to apply for asylum •
> to set a quota *(eine Quote festlegen)* • to strengthen border controls • restrictive immigration policy •
> to be a permanent resident *(einen ständigen Wohnsitz haben)* • to be naturalized *(eingebürgert werden)* •
> assimilation • integration • banner • torch • to melt into *(verschmelzen)* • melting pot *(Schmelztiegel)*

**2** a) The Push and Pull Theory tries to explain migration. On the one hand there are push factors that drive people away from a place and on the other hand there are pull factors that draw people to a place. Decide whether the following factors are push or pull factors, then put them in the box below.

> high unemployment rate • famine *(Hungersnot)* • good living conditions • better chances of finding a partner

b) Add additional factors.

| push factors | pull factors |
|---|---|
| | |
| | |
| | |
| | |
| | |

**3** One of the pull factors with regards to the U.S. is the idea of the American Dream, the dream of a better life, of infinite opportunities for everybody regardless of their origin. The Statue of Liberty is considered a symbol of welcome to all who come to the new world in search of a better life. There is a poem on its pedestal which is regarded as an epitome of this welcome.

a) What do you know about these figures? Compare them – what is similar, what is different?

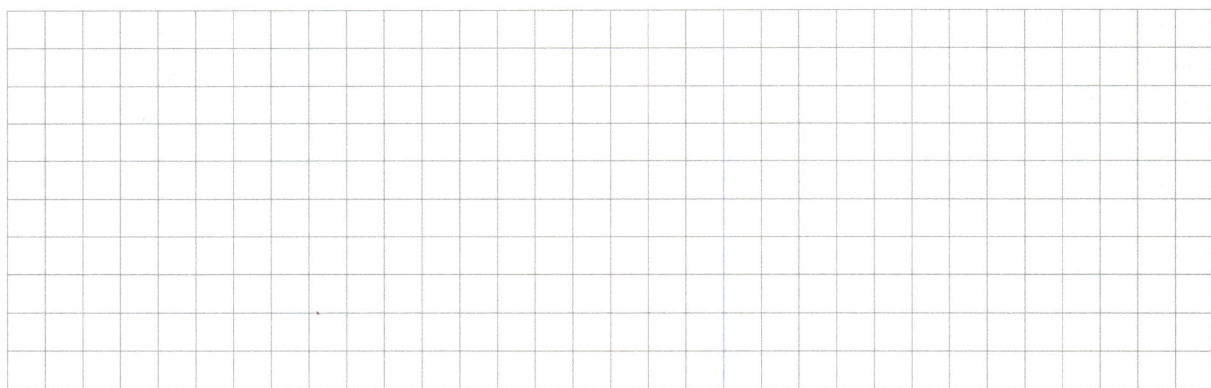

b) Close your eyes and listen to the audio of the poem by Emma Lazarus. What is it about? Which phrases stick in your mind?

🔊 **www.diesterweg.de/amb/04977/links**
→ The New Colossus

**The New Colossus**

Not like the brazen giant of Greek fame,
With conquering limbs astride from land to land;
Here at our sea-washed, sunset gates shall stand
A mighty woman with a torch, whose flame
5 Is the imprisoned lightning, and her name
Mother of Exiles. From her beacon-hand
Glows world-wide welcome; her mild eyes command
The air-bridged harbor that twin cities frame.
"Keep, ancient lands, your storied pomp!" cries she
10 With silent lips. "Give me your tired, your poor,
Your huddled masses yearning to breathe free,
The wretched refuse of your teeming shore.
Send these, the homeless, tempest-tost to me,
I lift my lamp beside the golden door!"

**brazen** – *metallen, aus Messing*
**astride** – *gespreizt*

**beacon** – *Leuchtfeuer*
**air-bridged** – space between New York and
    Brooklyn
**storied pomp** – *sagenumwobener Prunk*
**huddled** – *zusammengedrängt, hier:*
    *geknechtet*
**yearning** – *begehren, sich sehnend*
**wretched refuse** – *jämmerlicher Abfall*
**teeming** – *überfüllt*
**tempest-tost** – *vom Sturm Getriebene*

*Emma Lazarus*

c) Poetry circle

- Read the poem on your own. Look up vocabulary if necessary.
- Get into groups of three or four. Each group should pick one of the roles below.
- As a group, present your results to the class. The order of the presentations should follow the order of the roles as listed below.

**1. Illustrator**
Your job is to draw what you see when you hear the poem read aloud.

**2. Performing troop**
Your job is to recite and act out the poem. Why do you emphasise a line or a word?
Why do you leave a pause?

**3. Language lover**
Your job is to choose one or more of your favourite lines and share them with the group.
Give reasons for your selection.

**4. Image catcher**
Your job is to identify all of the literary images. Do they have a certain meaning?
What associations do the images have?

**5. Logician**
Your job is to determine the narrative logic of the poem. Is there a progression of ideas?

d) Write down 50 words why the poem has always appealed to people all over the world.

4   The following cartoon deals with immigration to the United States.

a) Look closely at the cartoon and circle five elements you think are important and should be described and interpreted. What do they show?

b) Exchange your ideas with a partner.

c) The following text was written by a student whose task it was to write a cartoon analysis. Read the text – does the student mention the most important aspects?

d) Read the analysis again and highlight expressions in the text that are useful for cartoon analysis.

*The cartoon was first published in Puck Magazine on June 2, 1909. It is entitled "The Fool Pied Piper." The cartoon shows Uncle Sam as the Pied Piper leading rats away from the European continent towards the United States with a pipe labeled "Lax Immigration Laws." The rats are labeled "murderer," "thief," "kidnapper," and "assassin." In the background you can see houses and a palace with the French, the Russian and the Italian flag on top. Outside the stylized city, European noblemen, politicians and citizens are standing on the shore cheering the piper.*

*The cartoonist satirizes the U.S. immigration policy of the time, implying that lax immigration laws encourage the immigration of people who pose a threat to society. He gets his message across by comparing Uncle Sam, the personification of the USA, with the Pied Piper of Hamelin, the protagonist of a popular legend in which a man with a pipe is hired by townspeople to lure away rats. In the legend, the piper is a clever and able man, who not only successfully rids the town of the rats, but also successfully takes revenge on the townspeople when they refuse to pay him. The piper in the cartoon, however, is a fool. He directs the rats towards his own country and doesn't seem to notice how dangerous they are. He isn't looking at the rats while piping, instead he is looking away from them. The rats are depicted as dangerous, with burning torches in their mouths, grim faces and notes with black hands alluding to the threat they pose to U.S. society. The local townspeople are happy to get rid of their rats. The cartoon implies that unlike the story of the Pied Piper of Hamelin, the citizens in the cartoon do not even have to hire someone, U.S. immigration law does the job for free.*

*The cartoonist uses techniques such as exaggeration, simplification, distortion and personification in order to achieve the desired effect. The consequences of the lax immigration laws of the time are grossly exaggerated. These laws might have made immigration for people with a criminal background easier, but they didn't work like a magic pipe. Another exaggeration and distortion is the way the rats are depicted. There is no doubt that some of the immigrants from Europe in the 19th century were petty criminals, but they were certainly less dangerous than they appear in the cartoon. Comparing Europe with a city that contains countries such as France, Italy and Russia is another effective simplification which is necessary for communicating the message.*

*In my opinion, the cartoonist conveys his message (that passing lax immigration laws leads to the immigration of unwanted people from Europe) effectively, especially by depicting immigrants as rats.*

**5** Study the cartoon *Looking Backward* (1893) by Joseph Keppler.
Use the boxes to describe and interpret the circled elements.

*Man with non-matching shadow*
↓
*The shadow alludes to his immigrant background*

*Different hats*
↓
*Immigrants come from different countries.*

LOOKING BACKWARD.
THEY WOULD CLOSE TO THE NEW-COMER THE BRIDGE THAT CARRIED THEM AND THEIR FATHERS OVER.

J. Keppler

---

to symbolize sth. • to allude to sth. *(auf etw. anspielen)* • to represent sth. • sb. is portrayed/depicted as … •
to indicate sth. *(auf etw. hinweisen)* • to refer to sth. *(sich auf etw. beziehen)* • the overall atmosphere is rather … •
due to the facial expression/gestures *(aufgrund des Gesichtsausdrucks/der Gesten)* • to be eye-catching •
the cartoonist wants to make the viewer aware of sth. • to exaggerate sth. *(etw. übertreiben)* •
by using/presenting …, the cartoonist intends to …

**6**   Fill in the boxes below as preparation for your analysis of the cartoon, *Looking backward*, on p. 65. Look at the text on p. 64 for helpful phrases.

| Introduction |
| --- |
| Important aspects (notes only) |
| |
| Helpful phrases |
| |

| Description |
| --- |
| Important aspects (notes only) |
| |
| Helpful phrases |
| |

| Interpretation |
| --- |
| Important aspects (notes only) |
| |
| Helpful phrases |
| |

| Evaluation |
| --- |
| Important aspects (notes only) |
| |
| Helpful phrases |
| |

**7**   Use your notes from task 6 to write an analysis of the cartoon.

📖 **How to analyze and interpret cartoons → see skills pp. 100-101**

**8**   a) Compare the message of the cartoon with the message of the poem, *The New Colossus* (p. 62).

b) Exchange your ideas with a partner.

**9** Sociologists have used different metaphors to explain how people of different origins and from different cultures live together in one society. Look at these examples of such metaphors. Read the text and explain in your own words how the images function as metaphors for American society.

melting pot

pizza

salad bowl

quilt

# U.S.-American society –
# a melting pot or a salad bowl?

All the terms above have been used to describe U.S.-American society. The melting pot metaphor – the oldest and most famous metaphor – reflects the idea of forming a new society consisting of people from various
5 backgrounds. According to the melting pot metaphor American society is made up of immigrants who have fully assimilated not only by marrying immigrants from other countries, but also by giving up the traditions and culture of their native countries. They have developed
10 an American way of life and an American identity, have adopted the English language and formed communities together with immigrants from other countries. This view of American society is expressed by the official motto of the U.S.: *e pluribus unum* (= out of many, one).
15 You can find this motto on the one-dollar bill and on the American coat of arms. The melting pot metaphor has often been criticized for not taking into account three major groups of Americans: Afro-Americans, Native Americans and immigrants from Southern and
20 Eastern Europe. However, applied to immigrants from Northern and Western Europe only, the metaphor can be regarded as adequate.

According to the salad bowl metaphor (sometimes other metaphors are used: bouquet, quilt or pizza),
25 U.S.-American society is made up of people with different backgrounds who do not merge into a homogenous culture but keep their own distinct identities. For instance, they cherish traditions of their native countries, are married to immigrants from the
30 same ethnic background, spend a lot of time among people from the same ethnic background and still speak the language of their native countries. What all these people have in common is that they live in the United States, usually speak English to some degree
35 and regard themselves as Americans. The salad bowl metaphor is similar to the European concept of multiculturalism.

## B – Focus on belonging

**1** a) The article below deals with the problems non-white Americans growing up and living in the U.S. have to face. The following words and phrases are taken from the article – use them to speculate about the article's content.

> hyphenated Americans  •  self identity  •  out-group status  •  subordinate  •  misguided notion  •  to be otherized

b) Skim the text. Were your speculations correct?

c) Translate the highlighted expressions. Write down your translations in the left column.

d) The following text is printed in ongoing lines. Set paragraphs using the following symbol ⌐.
Write down keywords in the right column that summarize the different paragraphs.
All in all there are 10 paragraphs, the first one has already been done for you.

**The Guardian**
**My least favourite question: where are you from?**
*Patricia Park*                                     *Friday 26 April 2013*

*personal: reason for the article*

As a non-white American, I'm often asked where I'm from and whether I've been "back home". And people don't mean New York City, where I was born and raised. They look at me, and my ethnic face, and they mean South Korea. ⌐ That was how I used to
5 answer, too. Even though I had never lived in South Korea until I was almost 30. Even though my parents were born in what is now North Korea, fled to the South as wartime refugees, then took the slow boat to Argentina, before becoming naturalized Americans. Despite the fact that I recited the pledge of allegiance at school
10 each morning, despite my blue US passport, I never self-identified as American while growing up; it had never occurred to me that I was. What I describe is hardly a new phenomenon: scores of fellow ethnic "others" have long felt similarly un-American growing up in the US, facing subtle rhetorical reminders of our
15 out-group status. It's well-trodden territory, treated in *My Big Fat Greek Wedding*, *The Joy Luck Club*, and the works of Chang-Rae Lee. As "hyphenated Americans", our identities are qualified – our Americanness is made subordinate, and secondary, to all the ethnic matter that precedes it. We are constantly told to
20 look to that other home, our "real" home, as the place where we truly belong. But what we have failed to address is the reverse phenomenon: what exactly awaits us when we "return" to the quote-unquote motherland. As a society we carry romantic notions of stepping off the plane – or boat – and being met with
25 open arms, perpetuated by the likes of Olive Garden commercials ("When you're here, you're family!") and even Jersey Shore, where Snooki et al set off for Italy to search for their roots under every pizza box and carafe of Chianti. Conan O'Brien famously parodied this romanticized attachment to the "old country"
30 when he traveled to Ireland and pressed his giant orange head into the bosom of each and every startled passerby, claiming kinship. It is wrong to assume that hyphenated-Americans can simply "return" to the "motherland" and automatically fit in. I, too, was once guilty of the same misguided notion, when I
35 traveled to Seoul as a Fulbright scholar to reconnect with my

*war time refugee – Kriegsflücht-linge*

ethnic identity. My parents left the Korean peninsula shortly after electricity came into vogue; as such, my cultural knowledge was at least 40 years out-of-date. Weaned on stories of my parents' war-torn childhood, I pictured straw-thatched houses dotting
40 the fields of rice paddies, and villagers gathering in the town square to kick around the old pigskin (a pig's bladder blown up like a soccer ball). I clung fiercely to this quaint, rustic (read: naïve) image of the old country. When I touched down in Korea, I was shocked to find the place that I thought I knew so intimately
45 – the place I was supposed to hail from – was so foreign. Great skyscrapers towered over the paved streets. Neon storefronts blinked advertisements for cell phones and fried chicken. My "kinsmen" – bedecked in suits and heels – jostled past me without a word, let alone greeting. Whenever I communicated in our
50 "native" tongue, the South Koreans laughed at my antiquated vocabulary (I peddled words like *apothecary*, *outhouse*) and my distinctly American cadence (I spoke in iambic pentameter). They said I was a "foreigner"; not one of "our country's people," the term they used to refer to themselves. Never did they call me
55 Korean. Once again I felt like the other – except this time, I was otherized by the ethnic group I was told my whole life I was a part of. There is a real danger in spending your whole life thinking you belong to some other place that's anywhere but here. My time abroad might have been less culturally wrought if I had never
60 tried to assume an automatic entitlement to Korea. What my experience in South Korea affirmed for me was that you can't go (back) home again – that home was never yours to lay claim to in the first place. I have since returned home, to New York City, with a newfound sense of orientation, and belonging. But it's
65 an uphill battle. I don't always feel American, especially on days when people insist on asking, "No, where are you *from* from?" or compliment my accent-free English. But we must challenge our views on hyphenated-Americans and their place of belonging. You might even say it's time we collectively weaned ourselves off
70 the proverbial teat of the motherland. Change is slow, and hard. But if we take even the smallest, simplest steps – like revising the rhetoric we use to talk about where we come from – the sooner Americans like myself might stop looking for acceptance over there, and start to feel we, too, have a claim to our real homeland
75 here in the United States.

**2** a) List the consequences of using hyphenated-terms like Korean-American as outlined by the author.

b) Get together with a partner and try to visualize your results in a drawing.

c) Talk to partner. Could there be a similar text about German society? What would be the same, what would be different?

## C – Focus on film

**Info box**

Migration: the process of moving from one place to another place within a country or between countries
Emigration: the process of leaving a country in order to settle in a different one
Immigration: the process of arriving in a new country in order to get settled there

**1** Note down examples of immigration in *Gran Torino*.

**2** Which of the facts in the text about the Hmong help you to reach a deeper understanding of the film? Explain.

**Hmong in Detroit (Michigan)**

The Hmong are one of the largest ethnic minority groups in Southeast Asia, mainly located in the mountainous regions of China, Vietnam, Laos, and Thailand. During the Vietnam War (1964 – 1973), especially in Laos, indigenious Hmong people were recruited by the USA to block supply lines from the Communist enemy and rescue downed American pilots. After the War, they became the target of Communist retaliation. Consequently,
5 some Hmong retreated to their villages, others fled to other countries. Today there are about 210,000 Hmong who reside in the USA. About 6000 live in Michigan, largely concentrated in the Detroit area, where they make up the majority of Detroit's Asian community.

The Hmong are concentrated in geographic locations to support the clan structure and to receive the support of the clan, a large family network. Hmong Americans are organized into an 18-clan structure; all members of a
10 clan recognize that they are related by a common ancestor. The family is a subcomponent of the clan structure. Membership of a clan is acquired through birth or marriage. It is not only a social category but also a spiritual designation, since the ancestral spirits watch over their family members.

The actions of individuals affect the reputation of the extended family. By tradition, the Hmong maintain strong family bonds that are based on interdependence rather than independence. As a result, it is expected that elders
15 will rely on the extended family for assistance, and that younger family members will put their personal desires behind the interests of the family.

When it comes to economic well-being in the United States, Hmong are among the least affluent Asian immigrant groups. Traditional familial obligations and immigrant parents who speak little English often make their high school careers difficult. Programs that are intended to boost integration and upward mobility are often slowed
20 down by racist sentiments. These sentiments are rooted in people feeling that immigrants pose a threat to white Americans' jobs. The decline of the auto manufacturing industry has made that dynamic particularly pronounced in Detroit.

| facts | explanation |
|---|---|
|  |  |

**3** Spider charts are a helpful way to display multiple data within one diagram. They show or compare strengths and weaknesses between different things. Normally there is a scoring range from 0 (in the center) to 5 (at the edge), with 5 indicating the highest level.

Diagram 1 visualizes the two concepts of the melting pot and the salad bowl. The concept of the melting pot, for example, suggests that people have completely adopted the American way of life and speak English fluently.

a) Explain the salad bowl concept as displayed in diagram 1.

### Diagram 1 – Melting pot and salad bowl

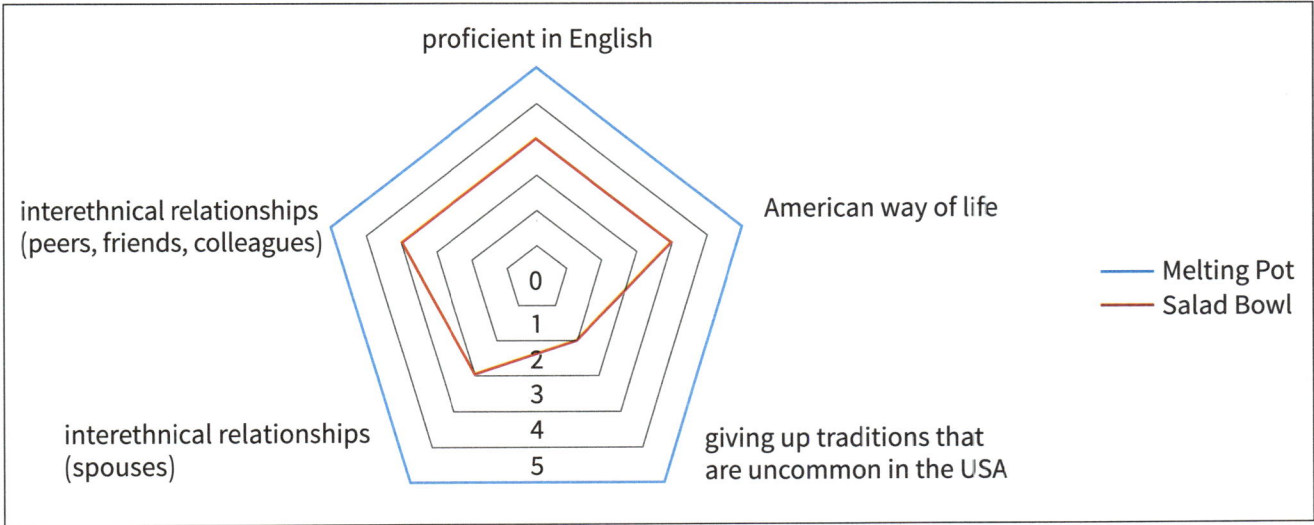

b) Examine the following characters from *Gran Torino* – Walt, Sue, Hmong grandmother – to determine where they range and fill out diagram 2.

c) Discuss which of the concepts above – the melting pot or the salad bowl – are more appropriate to illustrate present-day America.

### Diagram 2 – Characters from *Gran Torino*

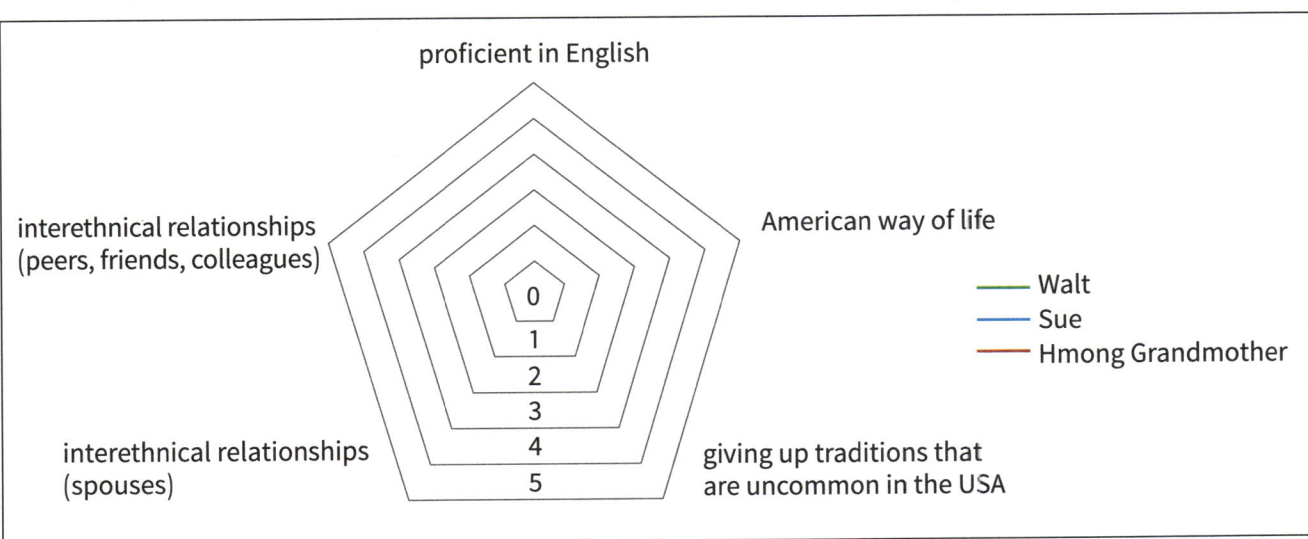

**4**  a) Read the following quote from Salman Rushdie.

> "The roots of self are the place that you know, the community that you come from, the language that you speak and the cultural assumptions within which you grow up. Those are the four great roots of the self and very, very often what happens to migrants is that they lose all four – they're in a different place, speaking an alien language, amongst people who don't know them and the cultural assumptions are very different. You can see that's something traumatic."

b) Explain the quote in your own words. The words in the box below might help you.

> to long to belong • to have a place to go • to maintain social ties • to be disconnected and uprooted • to suffer from loneliness • to feel excluded from • to isolate oneself from • to feel rootless • to experience uncertainty/insecurity • to be torn between • ambiguity

c) Rushdie mentions four roots of the self.

- What do they mean to you?
- What would Thao say? Exchange your ideas with a partner.

**5**  To Salman Rushdie, home is one of the roots of self, one component that establishes a sense of belonging. Choose a character from the film or the short story and explain why 'home' might be an ambiguous concept for them.

## A – Fundamental aspects

**1** Look at the pictures below. When do you think they are from? Give reasons for your answer.

**2** Listen to the background information about each picture and take notes. Add any questions you might have.

🔊 **www.diesterweg.de/amb/04977/links**
→ Picture descriptions

*when:* taken on school compound of
Little Rock, Arkansas in the 1950s
• school desegregated as a result of a Supreme
  Court decision
• as the picture shows, there was opposition to
  the enrollment of African-American students
*questions:* name of Supreme Court decision?
What is the National Guard?

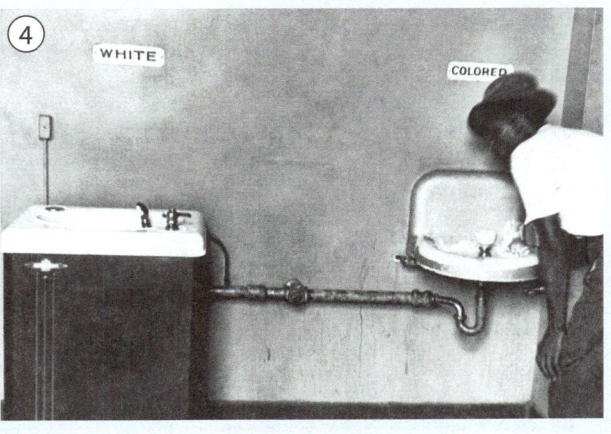

**3**   Look at the pictures on p. 73 again with a partner and …

- … exchange information about the pictures.
- … try to find answers to any questions you might have.
- … discuss what each picture tells you about black and white people in the United States at the time the pictures were taken/painted.

Use expressions from the wordbox below.

> to be full of contempt *(voller Verachtung sein)* • to be inferior/superior to sb. *(unterlegen/überlegen sein)* • evidence of hatred • a depiction of *(eine Darstellung von)* • to consider sth. legitimate • to exploit sb. • to be entitled to certain rights *(den Anspruch auf bestimmte Rechte haben)* • humiliation *(Erniedrigung)* • to humiliate sb. • considerable racial progress • racial minority • to exclude sb. from sth. • dignity • exploitation *(Ausbeutung)* • racial discrimination • to discriminate against sb. • white dominance • to be innately inferior *(von Natur aus unterlegen sein)* • to gain equal opportunity • to regard sb. as inferior • to claim superiority *(Überlegenheit beanspruchen)* • to be denied basic rights • segregation *(Rassentrennung)* • to fight for one's rights • to treat sb. with (dis)respect

**4**   Compare the picture below with the pictures on p. 73. Focus on the way African-Americans are portrayed and the roles they play in society.

> **Background Information**
> In the picture you can see Oprah Winfrey on the left. She is an American talk show host, media producer, actor and philanthropist. Born into poverty in Mississippi to a teenage single mother, she is now one of the most influential women in the world. The woman on the right is Michelle Obama, who published her autobiography entiteld *Becoming* in November 2018.

**5**  Read the following interpretation and, by taking the statistics below into consideration, find out which ethnic group it refers to.

"Throughout the complete period covered by the statistic, this group has fared better than many other groups. The line graph shows that the median household income among this group remained relatively stable from the 1960s to the beginning of the 1980s, then it rose considerably until the end of the 1990s. From then the median income has been on roughly the same level except for a brief decline as a result of the economic crisis of 2008."

**6**  Choose one of the statistics. Prepare a short presentation about the information which your statistic provides concerning African-Americans. Use expressions from task 5. Then present it to a partner.

**Statistic 1**

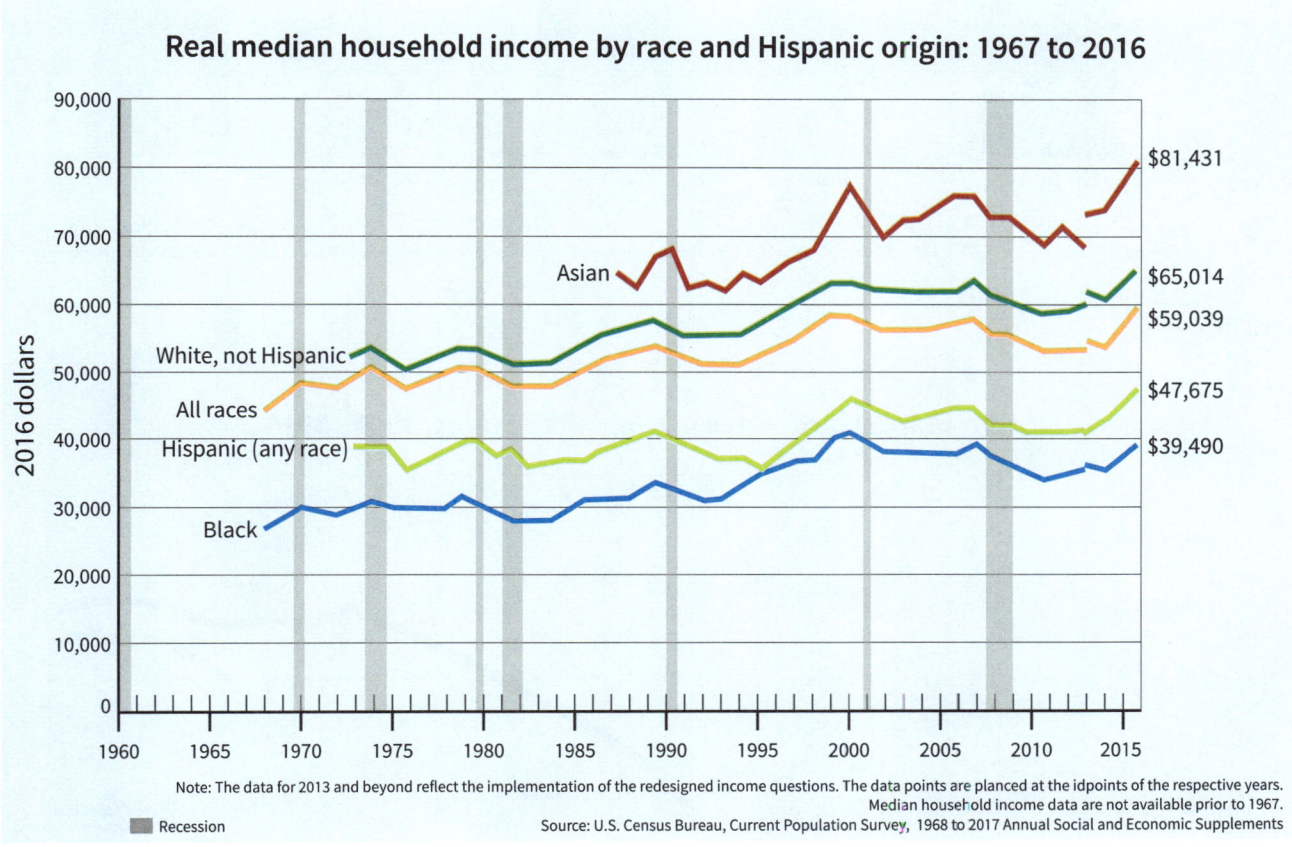

**Real median household income by race and Hispanic origin: 1967 to 2016**

Note: The data for 2013 and beyond reflect the implementation of the redesigned income questions. The data points are planced at the idpoints of the respective years. Median household income data are not available prior to 1967.

Recession                    Source: U.S. Census Bureau, Current Population Survey, 1968 to 2017 Annual Social and Economic Supplements

**Statistic 2**

### Educational Attainment of the Population by Race and Hispanic Origin

|  | Total | High school graduate or more | Some college or more | Associate's degree or more | Bachelor's degree or more | Advanced degree |
|---|---|---|---|---|---|---|
| White alone | 168,420 | 88.8% | 59.2% | 42.8% | 32.8% | 12.1% |
| Non-Hispanic White alone | 140,638 | 93.3% | 63.8% | 46.9% | 36.2% | 13.5% |
| Black alone | 25,420 | 87.0% | 52.9% | 32.4% | 22.5% | 8.2% |
| Asian alone | 12,331 | 89.1% | 70.0% | 60.4% | 53.9% | 21.4% |
| Hispanic (of any race) | 31,020 | 66.7% | 36.8% | 22.7% | 15.5% | 4.7% |

Source: U.S. Census Bureau, 2015 Current Population Survey

Statistic 3

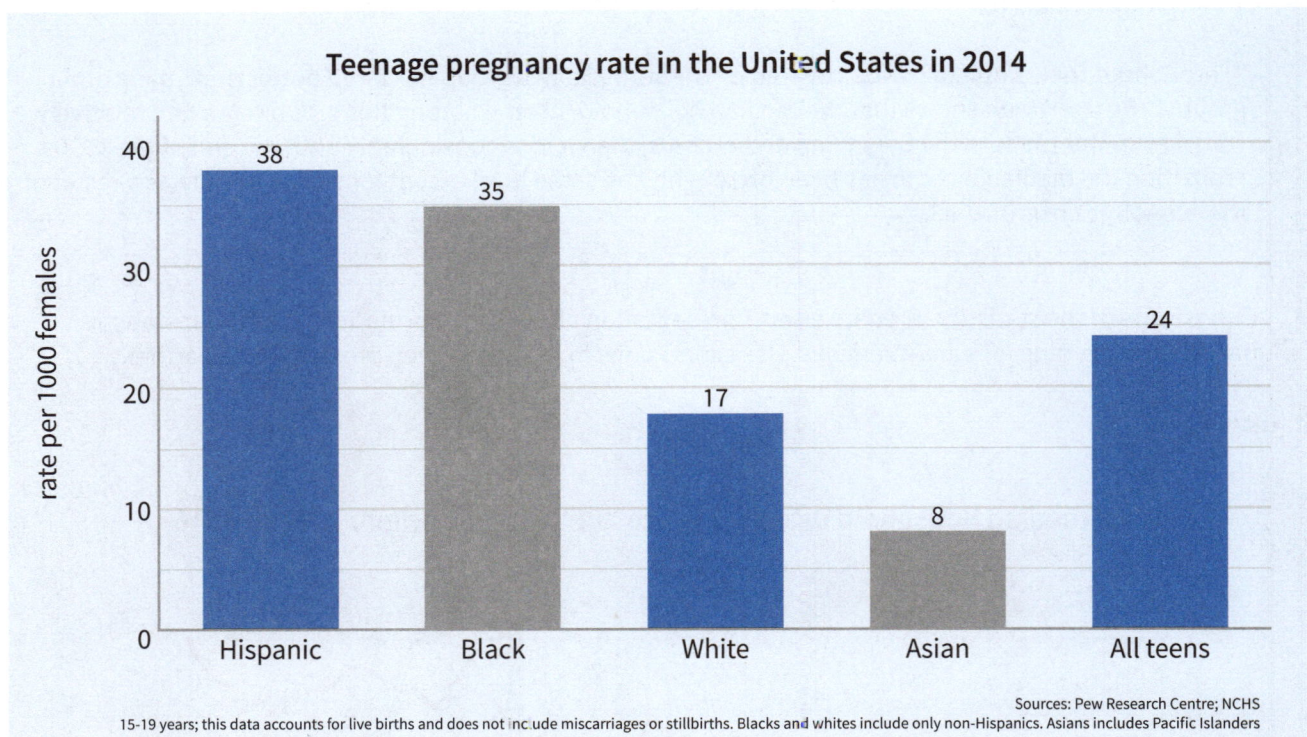

Teenage pregnancy rate in the United States in 2014
rate per 1000 females
40
30
20
10
0
38
35
17
8
24
Hispanic
Black
White
Asian
All teens
Sources: Pew Research Centre; NCHS
15-19 years; this data accounts for live births and does not include miscarriages or stillbirths. Blacks and whites include only non-Hispanics. Asians includes Pacific Islanders

Statistic 4

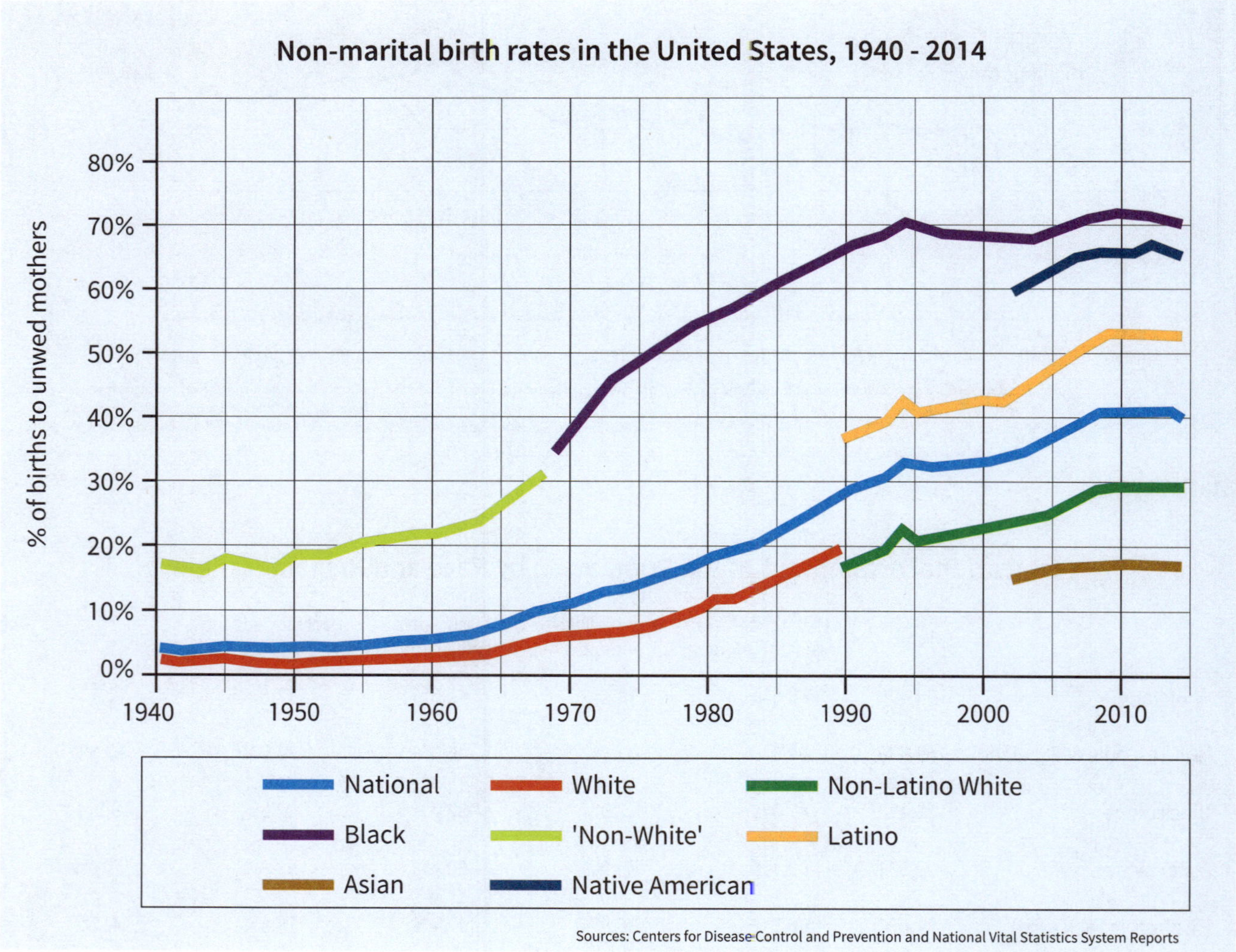

Non-marital birth rates in the United States, 1940 - 2014
% of births to unwed mothers
80%
70%
60%
50%
40%
30%
20%
10%
0%
1940
1950
1960
1970
1980
1990
2000
2010
National
White
Non-Latino White
Black
'Non-White'
Latino
Asian
Native American
Sources: Centers for Disease Control and Prevention and National Vital Statistics System Reports

**Affirmative action:** the practice of favoring individuals belonging to groups that have suffered past discrimination, also known as positive discrimination. An example in Germany would be the *Frauenquote*.

**7** Affirmative action – Partner 1:

a) Explain the cartoon to your partner and inform them about the opinions of the two bloggers below on affirmative action.

b) Discuss if affirmative action is an adequate way of righting the wrongs of the past, of meeting the challenge of racial inequality.

poor schooling, unconcious bias; wealth disparities, standardized tests

schools to prison pipeline; old boy network; underemployment

discrimination; racial profiling; disproportionate lifespan

privilege, connections, wealth

### Affirmative action reduces the wealth gap

Just look at the latest report on the wealth gap by the Urban Institute, it clearly shows that whites have passed on their wealth from generation to generation while most black families have never been wealthy and their children have never had the chance to go a prestigious university or start a business. We definitely need affirmative action, it is one way how we can close the wealth gap and give African-Americans a fair chance.

And on top of that, it's the only way to guarantee ethnic diversity at universities, something that a nation as diverse as the USA definitely needs. If we don't learn how we can peacefully live together with people of Hispanic or Asian or African origin at a young age, we'll keep our stereotypes and prejudices.

*posted on June 18th, by AlbertA*

### An African-American view on affirmative action

I have many white friends who show great interest in the debate over affirmative action and who look at affirmative action as a political issue. Yet for me as an African-American the significance is a different one: my family comes from Alabama and my ancestors have been discriminated against in many ways. My father was a gifted and hardworking student at school and he went to Alabama State University on a scholarship. Yet when my father had earned his degree (an MBA, Master's of Business Administration) and tried to apply for a job,  he was rejected in spite of his academic brilliance. He simply didn't have the same choices as white Americans. He finally found a badly-paid job in a small company run by an African-American in Montgomery. Affirmative action, for me, is a way to make up for the injustices of the past, that's why I support it.

*posted on June 19th, by WashingtonS*

**8** **Affirmative action – Partner 2:**

a) Explain the cartoon to your partner and inform them about the opinions of the two bloggers below on affirmative action.

b) Discuss if affirmative action is an adequate way of righting the wrongs of the past, of meeting the challenge of racial inequality.

**Affirmative action leads to injustice**

Some people say affirmative action has the potential to right the wrongs of the past. This might be true. What's ironic about these policies is that they are aimed at ending discrimination, and at the same time they discriminate against white males. Affirmative action is reverse discrimination. Don't get me wrong. I'm not saying we shouldn't think about ways to end racism. But affirmative action is unfair, because the racial or ethnic background of a person is not a qualification, it's simply a fact. And this fact shouldn't be taken into account when a person applies at a university or for a job.

*posted on June 2nd by admin*

**Affirmative action leads to stereotyping**

In the Declaration of Independence it says "We hold these truths to be self-evident that all men are created equal" and Martin Luther King has mentioned this phrase in his famous "I have a dream" speech. Equality also means equal treatment and affirmative action is unequal treatment. Affirmative action puts a label on African Americans: "you're a victim, you can't make it on your own." Let's stop victimizing blacks and let's get rid of affirmative action.

*posted on June 22nd by RonaldM*

## B – Focus on belonging

**1** a) On the right, you can see a picture which was taken during The Doll Experiment. Using this picture, speculate about what the scientists wanted to find out and how they did it.

b) Read the text about Mamie and Kenneth Clark's Doll Experiment and discuss the results, taking into consideration what you already know about race relations. Use expressions from the wordbox on p. 74.

### The doll experiment

In the early 1940s, American psychologists Mamie Clark and Kenneth Clark conducted an experiment with 253 Afro-American children to determine their attitude towards race. The children were aged between three and seven and came from different regions of the United States. The doll experiment involved a child being presented with two dolls. Both of these dolls were completely identical except for the skin and hair color. One doll was white with yellow hair, while the other doll was brown with black hair. The child was then given eight different instructions. The following table shows the results for requests 1 – 4.

| choice | request 1 (Give me the doll that you like to play with) | request 2 (Give me the doll that is a nice doll) | request 3 (Give me the doll that looks bad) | request 4 (Give me the doll that is a nice color) |
|---|---|---|---|---|
| Colored doll | 32 % | 38 % | 59 % | 38 % |
| White doll | 67 % | 59 % | 17 % | 60 % |
| Don't know or no response | 1 % | 3 % | 24 % | 2 % |

This experiment has often been repeated up to this day. The results were always similar showing deeply rooted prejudices.

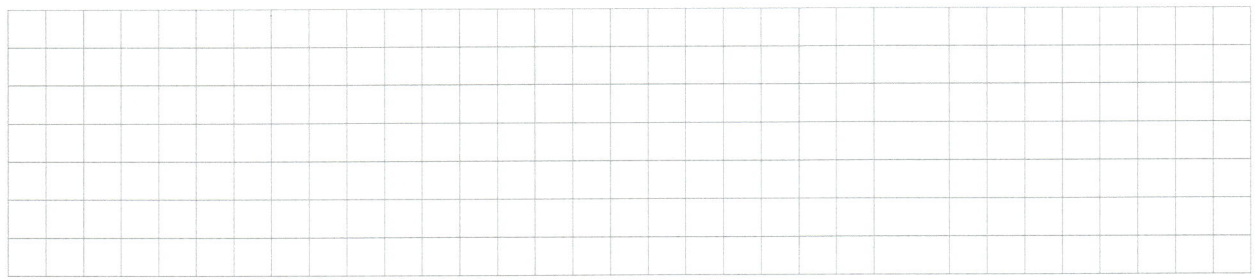

**2** In the text below, the author describes and reflects upon the ways Africans are treated in the USA in comparison to African Americans and what this means with regard to their identities. Use the following terms from the text to talk about possible differences between the way "Africans in America" and "African Americans" are treated by mainstream society.

> to be racially black • stereotypes • Harvard University • foreigner • to experience racism

**3** Read the text and highlight the passages which contain information about the differences between the way Africans and African Americans are treated and feel in the USA.

### The Guardian
### African in America or African American?
*Mūkoma wa Ngũgĩ*                                                        *14 January 2011*

"You do not know what it means to be black in this country," an American-born son told his African father. He was right. White America differentiates between Africans and African Americans, and Africans in the United States have generally accepted this differentiation. This differentiation, in turn, creates a divide
5 between Africans and African Americans, with Africans acting as a buffer between black and white America.

It is with relief that some whites meet an African. And it is with equal relief that some Africans shake the hand proffered in a patronising friendship. Kofi Annan, the Ghanaian former UN secretary general, while a student in the United States,
10 visited the South at the height of the civil rights movement. He was in need of a haircut, but this being the Jim Crow era, a white barber told him "I do not cut nigger hair." To which Kofi Annan promptly replied "I am not a nigger, I am an African." The anecdote, as narrated in Stanley Meisler's Kofi Annan: A Man of Peace in a World of War, ends with him getting his hair cut.

15 There are several interesting questions here. Why would Kofi Annan accept a haircut from a racist? Why did he not stand in solidarity with African Americans who, at that time, were facing lynching, imprisonment and other forms of violence simply for agitating for their rights? And equally intriguing, on what basis did the racist barber differentiate between African black skin and African American black
20 skin? Is an African not racially black? At a time of racial polarisation in the US, what made the haircut possible?

Being black and African, these are the types of questions with which I constantly wrestle as I navigate through myriads of confusing, illogical, but always hurtful and destructive racial mores. I was born in Evanston, Illinois to Kenyan parents.
25 We returned to Kenya when I was a few months old. I grew up in a small rural town outside of Nairobi, and attended primary and secondary school in Kenya before returning to the United States in 1990 for college. I have now lived in the United States half my life. What I have come learn is that in the United States, being African can get you into places being black and African American will not.

30 For instance, take the "African foreigner privilege". In Ohio, thirsting for a beer I walk into the closest bar. Silence. I order a beer and the white guy next to me says, "Where are you from? Where is your accent from?" I say, "Kenya." Relief, followed by the words "Welcome to America. I thought you were one of them." The thirsty writer in me is intrigued. Now that I am on the inside, I can ask "What do you mean?"
35 "Well, you know how they are," followed by a litany of stereotypes. Eventually, I say my piece but the guy looks at me with pity: "You will see what I mean." Never mind that to his "Welcome to America," I said I had been in the US for 20 years.

---

**Mūkoma wa Ngũgĩ** is the son of Ngũgĩ wa Thiong'o, a Kenyan writer who is world-famous for his plays, short stories, novels and essays.

**divide** – *Kluft*
**buffer** – *Puffer, Prellbock*

**relief** – *Erleichterung*
**patronising** – *gönnerhaft, herablassend*

**to agitate for sth.** – *sich für etw. einsetzen*
**intriguing** – *faszinierend, interessant*

**wrestle** – *ringen*
**myriads of** – *unzählige*
**mores (pl)** – *Sitten, Gebräuche*

**privilege** – *Vorrecht*

**litany** – *Litanei, endlose Aufzählung*

The end result of the African foreigner privilege, usually dispensed with condescension, is that Africans are becoming buffers between white and black
40 America. There is now a plethora of reports comparing African students to African American students. The conclusion is that if Africans fresh off the boat are doing better than African Americans who have been here for centuries, then racism can no longer be blamed. But the reports do not consider that, just maybe, at either Harvard or a community college, Africans experience race differently from African
45 Americans. Africans experience a patronising but helpful racism, as opposed to the hostile, threatened and defensive kind that African Americans grow up with. Racism wears a smile when meeting an African; it glares with hostility when meeting an African American. [...]

Indeed, Nelson Mandela once said that without African American support, ending
50 apartheid would have taken much longer. But one will not find organisations in African countries that reciprocate – for example, seeking to end a racialised judicial system in the US that sees more black men in prison than in college. And Africans in the United States tend to stay away from protests against police brutality and racial profiling. True, the fear of immigration police and offending
55 the host country play a part, but I think there are ways in which Africans do not see the African American struggle against racism as their fight, too.

Twenty years and counting in the US, I no longer feel a conflicted identity, one is that torn between being black in the United States and African. Going to Kenya this past December for the Kwani Literary Festival, I saw no contradiction between
60 going home to Kenya and returning home to the US. I do not fully comprehend terms like cosmopolitan. I do not float around in a universal home. But it makes sense to me that one can have two homes at the same time. Not just in the physical sense, but in the deepest sense of the word – to be rooted, and to have roots growing, in two different places.

65 And as a writer and citizen, I have duties to each. I want to open up the contradictions that, in Kenya, keep the majority in oppressive ethnicised poverty and violence and, in the United States, racialised violence and poverty.

As an African and a black person, I feel, rightly or wrongly, that I have a duty to love both homes. And love need not always be pleasant – it can be demanding,
70 defensive, angry and wrong, but it always wants to build, not destroy.

| | |
|---|---|
| **dispensed** – *austeilen, verteilen* | |
| **condescension** – *herablassende Haltung* | |
| **plethora** – *Fülle* | |
| **hostile** – *feindselig* | |
| **reciprocate** – *sich revanchieren* | |
| **struggle** – *Kampf* | |
| **and counting** – *und mehr* | |
| **torn between** – *hin- und hergerissen zwischen* | |
| **contradiction** – *Widerspruch* | |
| **rooted** – *verwurzelt* | |
| **duty** – *Pflicht* | |
| **pleasant** – *angenehm* | |

**4** In line 35, the white person in the bar tells the author "Well, you know how they are." On the basis of what you know about the relationship between African Americans and whites, write down what the white man in the bar possibly thought of when he said "Well, you know how they are."

**5** When the author tells the story of Kofi Annan asking for a haircut (l. 8), he wonders on what basis the barber "differentiates between African black skin and African American black skin." In the passages following the anecdote, the author provides possible answers to this question. Highlight these answers.

**6** The following factors – among others – can shape people's sense of belonging:

1. country of birth / country of residence, 2. skin color      3. history, 4. relationship to mainstream society
                    **(Partner A)**                                                                **(Partner B)**

Work with a partner. Partner A takes factors 1 and 2, partner B takes factors 3 and 4. Explain how these factors shape the sense of belonging of Africans and African-Americans in the USA according to the author. Also identify situations mentioned in the text in which people feel ambiguous about where they belong.

## C – Focus on short story

**1** Read through *The child* again and highlight all the information you can find on the economic status and the educational attainment of the African-American characters in the story. Then write down your findings in the box below.

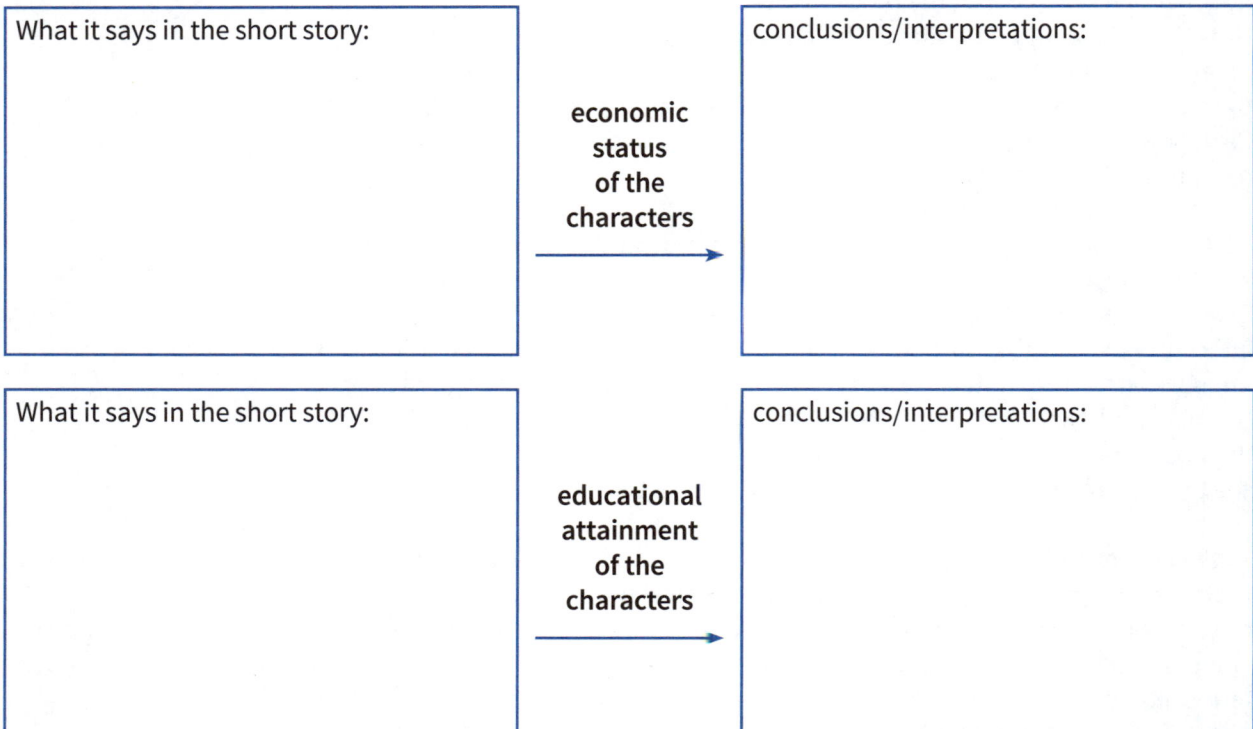

| What it says in the short story: | economic status of the characters → | conclusions/interpretations: |

| What it says in the short story: | educational attainment of the characters → | conclusions/interpretations: |

**2** Examine if your findings correspond to the information about the economic situation and the educational attainment of African-Americans in general.

**3** **Presentations**

**Partner A:** Karen thinks a lot about the drunk black man who is riding on the train with her. Analyze her thoughts about the black man and explain what her thoughts tell the reader about Karen's attitude towards being an African American. Take notes and then present your findings to a partner.

**Partner B:** Karen thinks a lot about the white girl who is riding on the train with her. Analyze her thoughts about the white girl and explain what her thoughts tell the reader about Karen's attitude towards being an African American. Take notes and then present your findings to a partner.

**4** Discuss which of the following adjectives best describe Karen's racial identity:

ambiguous  ·  insecure  ·  proud  ·  indifferent  ·  self-conscious

① The 2nd Amendment
A well regulated militia, being necessary to the security of a free state, the right of the people to keep and bear arms, shall not be infringed

WE SELL HOME & PERSONAL SECURITY LOW GUN PRICES WE BUY USED GUNS SHOP LOCAL

## A – Fundamental aspects

**1** a) What do the images above tell you about gun culture in the U.S.? Talk to a partner.

b) Work in groups. Collect what you know about gun culture in the U.S. in general.

> (fire) arms *(Schusswaffen)* • to carry guns • to be familiar with • gun owner • to run amok • proponent/opponent • to oppose • victim • to infringe sth. *(einschränken)* • gun ownership • gun control • to bear arms • militia *(Bürgerwehr)*

**2**   a) Read the following text, then complete the exercises on p. 86.

**Zeit Online**
**Warum die Amerikaner ihre Waffen so lieben**
*Eric T. Hansen*                                                           *24. Juli 2012*

**Wir Amerikaner lieben unsere Waffen, und daran sind die Europäer schuld.**

Es fing vor mehr als 250 Jahren an. Damals herrschte in Europa noch das
mittelalterliche Prinzip: Nur der Adel darf Waffen tragen. Zwar leisteten sich
schon manche Länder so etwas Neuartiges wie ein stehendes Heer, in dem
5 auch ausgewählte Mitglieder des Pöbels im Umgang mit Waffen trainiert
wurden. Dennoch blieben Waffen insgesamt Sache der Obrigkeit.

In Amerika gab es keine solchen Gesetze. Im Gegenteil: Das Land war Wildnis.
Man brauchte zum Überleben eine Waffe. Der größte Teil der Bevölkerung war
bewaffnet, Frauen und Kinder eingeschlossen.

10 Diese existenzielle Beziehung zur Waffe setzte sich im wilden Westen fort, und
der Westen war noch bis in die frühen Jahre des 20. Jahrhunderts wild. Das ist
gar nicht so lange her. Im Süden und im Westen ist der Umgang mit der Waffe
immer noch ein Symbol der Eigenständigkeit und für junge Männer auch ein
Schritt ins Erwachsenenalter.

15 In den Medien – in Amerika wie auch in Deutschland – wird der amerikanische
Waffenbesitzer meist als primitiver Redneck dargestellt. Davon gibt es
ja auch genug. Der durchschnittliche Waffenbesitzer aber sieht eher aus
wie mein Vater. Er wuchs in einer Holzhütte tief im Westen im ländlichen
Washington State an der Grenze zu Kanada auf. Es war mitten in der Großen
20 Depression, als die gesamte Wirtschaft um ihn herum zusammenbrach und
die Arbeitslosigkeit teilweise bis auf 30 Prozent stieg.

**Nur die Waffen ließen viele Amerikaner überleben**

Zum Glück lebten er und sein Vater am Rande eines Waldes. Wurde das Essen
rar, nahmen sie ihre Gewehre – mein Vater die Schrotflinte, sein Vater sein
25 Gewehr aus dem Ersten Weltkrieg – gingen in den Wald und kamen mit Hasen,
Eichhörnchen und Vögeln wieder heraus. Illegal, versteht sich. So haben sie
überlebt. So haben viele Amerikaner überlebt.

Als er dann in der Armee war und im Zweiten Weltkrieg in Übersee diente,
machte er mit anderen Waffen Bekanntschaft und brachte ein paar davon mit
30 zurück. Waffen begleiteten ihn sein ganzes Leben lang. Sie waren auch Teil
unserer Erziehung.

Es war ihm wichtig, dass wir Jungs wussten, mit Gewehren umzugehen.
Wie man sie trägt, hält, wie man sie sicher aufbewahrt. Er brachte uns den
Unterschied zwischen Spiel und Ernst bei, lehrte uns, dass man mit manchen
35 Dingen niemals spaßt. Als er starb, bekam ich die alte Schrotflinte. Das macht
mich zu einem der rund 80 Millionen Amerikanern, die Waffen besitzen.

Meine deutschen Freunde fragen oft: "Warum könnt ihr nicht strengere
Waffengesetze einführen wie bei uns? Ihr seht doch, dass es hier funktioniert."
Sie haben Recht: Die Mordrate in Westeuropa ist erheblich geringer als in
40 Amerika, und das hat wahrscheinlich auch etwas mit den Waffengesetzen

*right to carry arms:
Europe → only authorities*

*U.S. → everyone*

zu tun. Auf jeden Fall gibt es zu viele Waffen in Amerika. Nicht nur ich sage das. Etwas mehr als 40 Prozent der Amerikaner wollen heute schärfere Waffengesetze.

In den 1960ern fing man konsequent an, auch bei uns strengere Waffengesetze
45 einzuführen. Nur leider haben diese die Mordrate nicht nach unten getrieben. Im Gegenteil, sie stieg bis in die Neunziger weiter an.

Fiele die Statistik etwas eindeutiger zugunsten der Waffenkontrolle aus, wäre es vielleicht leichter, die National Rifle Association (NRA) und die anderen Waffenlobbys zu entmachten. Doch seit den 1990ern werden die
50 Waffengesetze immer lockerer, und gleichzeitig fällt ausgerechnet seit dieser Zeit die Mordrate immer tiefer.

Warum auch immer das so ist: Unter diesen Umständen wäre es selbst für Präsident Barack Obama oder seinen Herausforderer Mitt Romney schwer, von einem überzeugten Waffenfreund zu verlangen, er solle seine Waffe
55 abgeben. Das ist einer der Gründe, warum sie zu diesem Thema schweigen . Doch der wichtigste ist: Ob wir es wollen oder nicht, historisch gesehen waren es Waffen, die uns zu Amerikanern machten.

### Die Verfassung garantiert das Recht auf Waffenbesitz

Als wir 1776 den englischen Adel abschütteln wollten, konnten wir uns nur
60 deswegen behaupten, weil so gut wie jeder Mann zu Hause eine Knarre hatte. Die Demokratie wurde tatsächlich von lauter kleinen Privatarmeen erkämpft.

Nach der Unabhängigkeit fragten sich viele, wie lange es wohl dauern würde, bis die neue Regierung in Washington ebenfalls zu einer Tyrannei mutiert (von Anfang an waren wir paranoid, was das Verhältnis zur Obrigkeit angeht).
65 Um dem vorzubeugen, schrieb man schon ein paar Jahre später den zweiten Verfassungszusatz , der garantiert, dass der Privatmensch Waffen tragen darf. Es kann ja sein, dass er irgendwann eine Armee bilden muss.

Waffenkritiker meinen, der zweite Verfassungszusatz sei überholt (oder wäre aus heutiger Sicht einfach falsch interpretiert), und sie könnten Recht haben.
70 Deshalb ging die Frage vor einigen Jahren vor den Obersten Gerichtshof, der die endgültige Entscheidung traf: Der zweite Verfassungszusatz garantiert tatsächlich, dass jeder Amerikaner, und wenn er der letzte Depp ist, eine Waffe besitzen darf.

### Das Gewaltmonopol des Staates existiert in den USA nicht

75 Die Entscheidung des Obersten Gerichtshofes wird von Waffengegnern als ein tragischer Sieg der Rechten dargestellt, aber das Ganze reicht viel tiefer.

Mit dem zweiten Verfassungszusatz wurde 1791 die Bewaffnung des kleinen Mannes gegenüber der Obrigkeit festgeschrieben. In Deutschland spricht man gern vom "Gewaltmonopol des Staates": In den USA existiert dieses Monopol
80 nicht, und auch wenn es heute arg veraltet klingt, ist das seit 1776 ein Teil unseres Selbstverständnisses.

Deswegen legen wir die Waffe auch nicht aus der Hand, selbst wenn wir uns damit ins eigene Bein schießen.

b) Find the suitable translations for the highlighted words. To do so use the dictionary entries below.

**behaupten** [bəˈhauptən] **I.** *vt* ❶ *(äußern)* to claim; ■ **von jdm ~ , dass …** to say of sb. that …; ■ **es wird behauptet, dass …** it is said that … ❷ *(aufrechterhalten)* to maintain; **seinen Vorsprung gegen jdn ~** to maintain one's lead over sb. **I.** *vr* ■ **sich** *akk* **~** to assert oneself (**gegen** + *akk* over); **sich gegen die Konkurrenz ~ können** to be able to survive against one's competitors

**eher** [ˈeːə] *adv* ❶ *(früher)* sooner ❷ *(wahrscheinlicher)* more likely ❸ *(mehr)* more ❹ *(lieber)* rather

**ein|schließen** [ainˈʃliːsən] *vt irreg* ❶ *(in einem Raum schließen)* ■ **jdn ~** to lock sb. up ❷ *(wegschließen)* ■ **etw ~** to lock sth. away ❸ *(einbegreifen)* ■ **jdn ~** to include sb. ❹ *(einkesseln)* ■ **jdn/etw ~** to surround sb./sth.

**erheblich** [-ˈheːplɪç] **I.** *adj* ❶ *(beträchtlich)* considerable; *Nachteil, Vorteil* great; *Störung, Verspätung* major; *Verletzung* serious ❷ *(relevant)* relevant **II.** *adv* considerably

**um|gehen**[1] [ʊmˈgeːən] *vi irreg sein* ❶ *(behandeln)* to treat; **mit jdm nicht ~ können** to not know how to handle sb.; **mit etw** *dat* **gleichgültig/vorsichtig ~** to handle sth. indifferently/carefully ❷ *Gerücht* to circulate
**umgehen**[2] [ʊmˈgeːən] *vt irreg (vermeiden)* to avoid

**Hand** <-, Hände> [hant] *f* ❶ ANAT hand; **Hände hoch!** hands up!; **linker/rechter ~** on the left/right; **jdm etw in die ~ drücken** to press sth. into sb.'s hand; **jdm die ~ geben** to shake sb.'s hand; **etw in die ~ nehmen** to pick up sth.; **Hände weg!** hands off! ❷ *kein pl* SPORT *(Handspiel)* handball ❸ *(Besitz)* hands; **der Besitz gelangte in fremde Hände** the property passed into foreign hands
▷ WENDUNGEN: **die Hände in den Schoß legen** to sit back and do nothing; **[bei etw** *dat***] die Hände im Spiel haben** to have a hand in sth.; **bei jdm in besten Händen sein** to be in safe hands with sb.; **aus erster/zweiter ~** first-hand/second-hand; **jds rechte ~ sein** to be sb.'s right-hand man; **etw aus der Hand legen** to lay sth. down

| German | English translation (here) |
|---|---|
| *eingeschlossen* (l. 9) | |
| *eher* (l. 17) | |
| *umzugehen* (l. 32) | |
| *erheblich* (l. 39) | |
| *behaupten* (l. 60) | |
| *aus der Hand legen* (l. 82) | |

c) Write down the key aspects of the text in English in the blue column to the right of the text. Work with a partner. Summarize the text orally by taking turns and using your keywords.

d) Answer the following post published in a forum for exchange students. Use the information from the article.

I hope you all arrived safely in your families. I am really enjoying my first weeks and I have learned a lot already. But I am really irritated about one thing. My family has several weapons at home and last weekend they even took me to a shooting range. Are they gun crazy?

*Pierre from Paris, France*

# B – Focus on belonging

**1** Watch the clip in which Tom Franklin, a well-known U.S. writer, talks about his hunting experiences and answer the following questions.

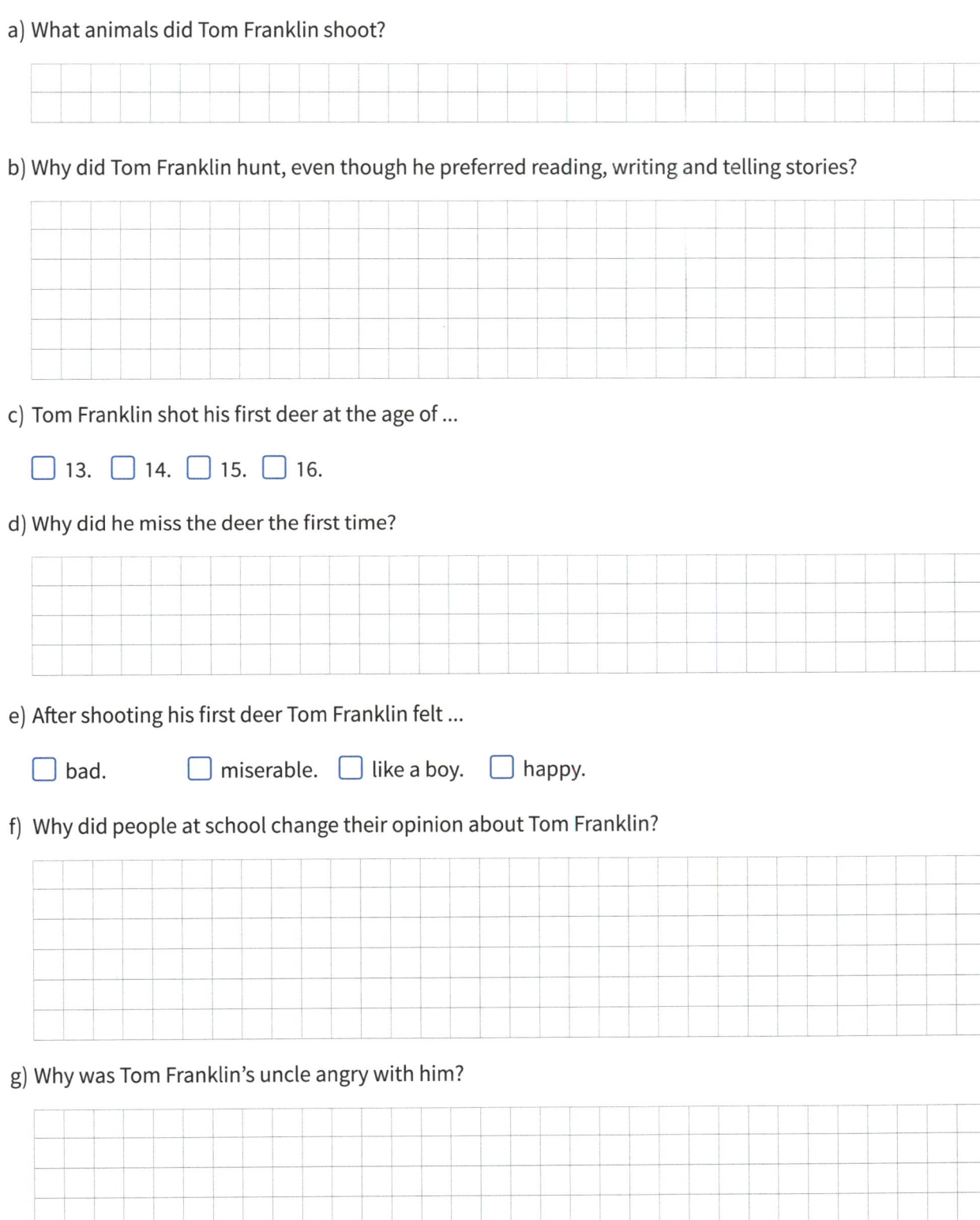

📹 **www.diesterweg.de/amb/04977/links**
→ Franklin on guns

a) What animals did Tom Franklin shoot?

b) Why did Tom Franklin hunt, even though he preferred reading, writing and telling stories?

c) Tom Franklin shot his first deer at the age of ...

☐ 13.  ☐ 14.  ☐ 15.  ☐ 16.

d) Why did he miss the deer the first time?

e) After shooting his first deer Tom Franklin felt ...

☐ bad.   ☐ miserable.   ☐ like a boy.   ☐ happy.

f) Why did people at school change their opinion about Tom Franklin?

g) Why was Tom Franklin's uncle angry with him?

**2** The article *Warum die Amerikaner ihre Waffen so lieben* on pp. 84-85 does not mention that weapons and their use can create a sense of belonging.

a) Talk to a partner: Where in the article would you include a paragraph about this aspect? Give reasons.

> personally, I (don't) feel/think/believe (that) • my personal opinion is that • to be honest I •
> I am convinced that • I guess • to be honest I • in my experience • from my perspective •
> I reckon • as far as I am concerned • speaking for myself • I have to admit • well, the point is •
> because • that is why • therefore • so • I'd say • on account of • as a consequence/result •
> as far as I can see • I suppose • I would say • I'm sure • let me add • basically, • I strongly believe

– Where?

– Why?

b) Write the additional paragraph for the article in English.

## C – Focus on film

**1**   a) Watch the following scenes and analyze the significance of guns in Walt's life. Take notes.

Scene "Maybe so father" (18:20 – 20:04)

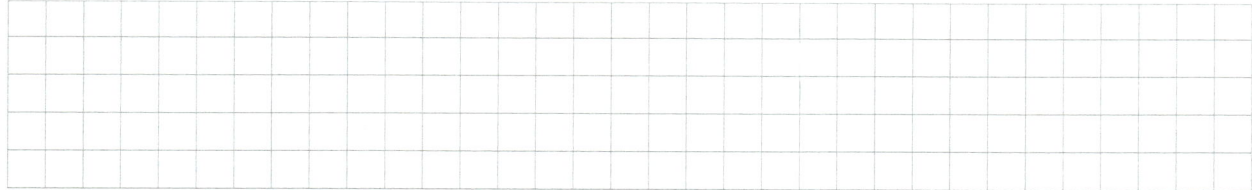

Scene "What the hell is this" (24:33 – 24:46)

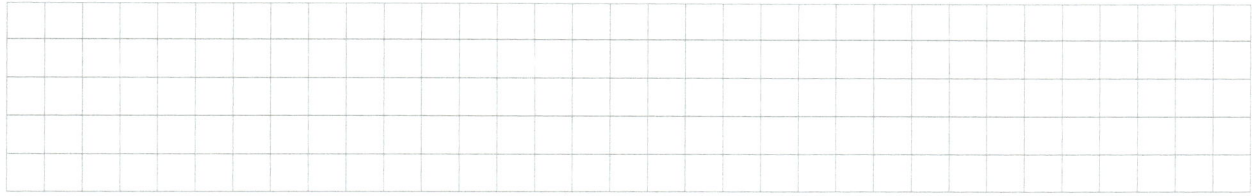

Scene "What the hell is this" 2 (25:40 – 26:10)

Scene "Get in the truck" (31:38 – 34:25)

Scene (01:34:42 – 01:37:17)

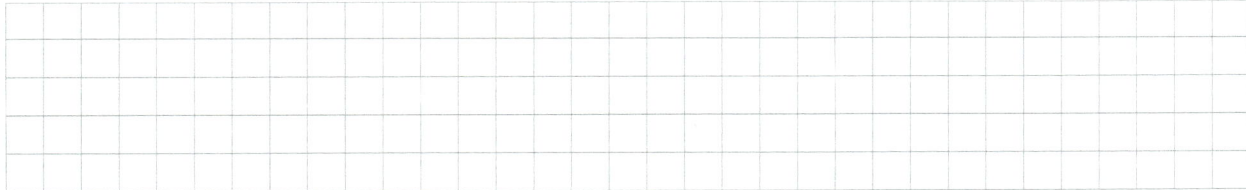

b) Look at your findings and draw a conclusion.

**2**    Read the following conversation between Walt and Father Janovich. Use it to explain why Walt's relationship with guns can be called ambiguous.

> **FATHER JANOVICH**
> Good afternoon, Walt.
> **WALT**
> I told you I'm not going to confession ...
> **FATHER JANOVICH**
> Why didn't you just call the police?
> **WALT**
> What?
> **FATHER JANOVICH**
> I do work with some of the Hmong gangs and I heard there was some trouble in the neighborhood. Why didn't you call the police?
> **WALT**
> Well ... You know why, I've prayed that they would show up, but ... nobody answered.
> **FATHER JANOVICH**
> What were you thinking? Someone could have been killed. We're talking life and death here.
> **WALT**
> When things go wrong, you gotta act quickly. When we were in Korea and a thousand screaming gooks came across our land ... we didn't call the police. We reacted.
> **FATHER JANOVICH**
> We are not in Korea, Mr. Kowalski, I've been thinking about our conversation on life and death.
>
> About what you said. About how you carry around all the horrible things you were forced to do. Horrible things that won't leave you. It seems that it would do you good to unload some of that burden. Things done during war are terrible. being ordered to kill ... killing to save yourself, killing to save others. You're right, those are things I know nothing about. But I do know about forgiveness. And I've seen a lot of men who have confessed their sins, admitted their guilt and left their burdens behind them. Stronger men than you! Men at war who were ordered to do appalling things ... and are now at peace.
> **WALT**
> Well I got to hand it to you, padre, you came here with your guns loaded this time. Thank you! – And you're right about one thing. About stronger men than me, reaching their salvation. Well, Hallefuckinlujah. – But you are wrong about something else.
> **FATHER JANOVICH**
> What's that, Mr. Kowalski?
> **WALT**
> The thing that haunts a man the most is what he isn't ordered to do.

**3**    Compare the significance of guns for Walt with the significance they have for the gangs. Take notes and talk to a partner.

**4**    Go back to the article *Warum die Amerikaner ihre Waffen so lieben* on pp. 84-85. Relate the film to the article and find examples for the central ideas.

# A – The Ambiguity of Belonging in general

**1**  a) Look at the pictures above. Write down your associations in the respective boxes below. The following expressions might help you.

> to bond with *(eine Verbindung eingehen mit)* • to differ from • to be identical • to feel included/excluded • to integrate into • to feel alienated *(entfremdet)* • to be torn between • to have mixed feelings about • to feel loyal to • to be hesitant *(zögerlich)* • to break bonds • to join • to participate in *(teilnehmen)*

| Picture 1 | Picture 2 |
|---|---|
|  |  |

| Picture 3 | Picture 4 |
|---|---|
|  |  |

b) You and a partner have to give a presentation on the topic of the *Ambiguity of Belonging* aimed at students your age. Discuss which of the illustrations above you could use. Try to come to an agreement.

## B – Focus on belonging

**1**  **Key issues of belonging**

a) Take the perspective of Karen from the short story *The child*. Look at the list of factors below that are all related to belonging. Choose three and be prepared to explain why these factors are the most prominent ones for Karen. Exchange your results with a partner.

| | | |
|---|---|---|
| acceptance | growth | loneliness |
| alienation | heritage | rebellion |
| change | identification | relationships |
| closeness | identity | (self) perception |
| community | inclusion | setting |
| development | individuality | sharing |
| ego | involvement | solitude |
| exclusion | isolation | understanding |

b) Choose at least one character from the film *Gran Torino* and do the same.

**2**  **Symbols and belonging**

Work with a partner: Choose symbols for each character and discuss in what way they express a certain sense of belonging for them.

**Walt:**  flag, Gran Torino, Medal of Honor, dog, beer, porch, gun

**Karen:**  book, student pass, baby bump

## 3 Characters and their need to belong

Below you will find typical key features of the need to belong.

a) Choose characters from the short story and from the film and decide which and how these aspects apply to them.

**General features of belonging:**

- the quality of interactions is more important to us than the quantity of interactions
- people hesitate to break bonds, even harmful ones
- the feeling of (not) belonging shapes our identity (and vice versa)

**Benefits of belonging: People are more likely to …**

- feel happy, calm, satisfied, balanced, stable etc.
- be able to cope with painful emotions more easily.
- be enabled to love themselves and others.

**Effects of not-belonging: People are more likely to …**

- suffer from psychological problems, such as loneliness, anxiety, jealousy, depression, grief, low self-esteem, mental distress etc.
- have behavioral problems, such as criminality, or may even commit suicide.
- develop a strong desire to form new relationships.
- develop a strong desire to exclude oneself.

b) Choose one feature from each category and illustrate it with an example from your life or from somebody else's life.

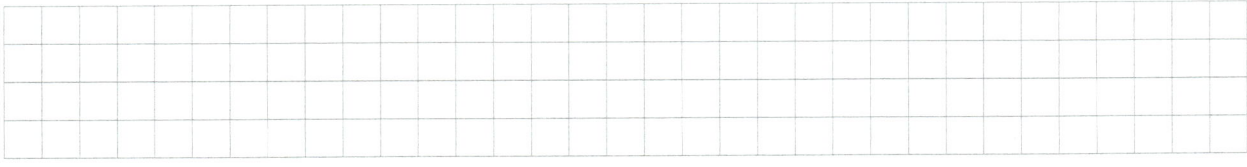

93

## C – Focus on Ambiguity

### 1 Core values and ambiguity

Core values articulate what we stand for, govern personal relationships, guide business processes, guide us on how we teach, and influence our decision making process.

a) In the following you will find a list of core values.
   For each character tick ☑ the ones that are important to them.

|  | Walt | Thao | Karen |
|---|---|---|---|
| honesty |  |  |  |
| dignity |  |  |  |
| love |  |  |  |
| family loyalty |  |  |  |
| achievements |  |  |  |
| wisdom |  |  |  |

|  | Walt | Thao | Karen |
|---|---|---|---|
| faith |  |  |  |
| optimism |  |  |  |
| wealth |  |  |  |
| kindness |  |  |  |
| self-determination |  |  |  |
| independence |  |  |  |

b) Find and analyze situations where core values come into conflict with one another.

c) Analyze Thao's sense of belonging before he met Walt and at the end of the film.
Fill in the table below.

| before he met Walt | at the end of the film |
| --- | --- |
|  |  |

**2** The characters and Ambiguity of Belonging in a nutshell

Fill in the table for the characters from *Gran Torino* and *The child*.

| Character | Why is their sense of belonging ambiguous? | Chosen strategies to deal with these ambiguities | Is the outcome satisfying for the character? | Alternative solutions? Chance to solve them? |
|---|---|---|---|---|
| | | | | |

Use this page to note down interesting things you have learnt from each chapter. This could be new information, new vocabulary and phrases or a reminder to yourself about a topic you would like to learn more about.

| 1 – The Ambiguity of Belonging |
| --- |
| |

| 2 – The child |
| --- |
| |

| 3 – Gran Torino |
| --- |
| |

| 4.1 – Family |
| --- |
| |

| 4.2 – The American Dream |
| --- |
| |

| 4.3 – Immigration |
| --- |
| |

| 4.4 – Race |
| --- |
| |

| 4.5 – Gun Culture |
| --- |
| |

# Statistics

Statistics collect, organize and present complex data in different forms. The most common forms are line graphs, tables, bar charts and pie charts. The focus of the presentation determines the choice of statistical representation. Line graphs, for example, can show developments over a period of time, tables present raw data, bar charts compare two or more figures and pie charts show percentages of 100%.

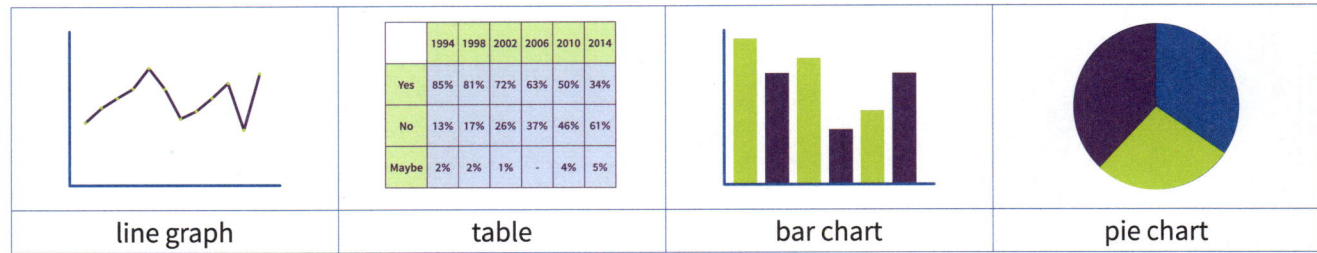

| line graph | table | bar chart | pie chart |

**Instruction: analyze, interpret**     ✓

**Writing process**

**Preparation**
- First, study the graph, the chart or the table carefully.
- Look at the title and the key thoroughly and highlight any interesting features.
- Note down central aspects as well as ideas on how to interpret the numbers.
- Check the reliability of the source and whether the numbers are up-to-date.

**Introduction**
- Identify the formal components of the presentation (table, chart, graph) and the period of time covered.
- Mention the origin/source, the author and the date.
- In one sentence, outline what the statistic depicts in general.

**Description**
- Outline the information it gives.
- Describe the developments/changes over time.
- Describe peaks and lows.
- Describe relationships and connections.
- Describe in a systematic way (e.g. mention the most important aspects first) and concentrate on the most remarkable data.
- Consider why the data is presented in a table, chart or diagram.

**Interpretation/Conclusion**
- Draw conclusions from the numbers.
- Relate the data to the given context and explain your conclusions with background knowledge of the topic.
- Be critical about the form of the presentation: e.g. Is it easily understandable? Is it a reliable source? Are there up-to-date numbers?
- Are the figures presented in a positive, negative or neutral light?
- Put your findings into a larger context.
- Draw a conclusion.

**Evaluation**
- Assess whether the statistic is effective in bringing across its message.

**Editing**
Read through your text. Check for ...
- common mistakes (spelling, grammar, punctuation).
- variety in vocabulary used (use a dictionary for help).
- readability (e.g. complex sentences).
- repetition.
- a reasonable, coherent structure.

| | ✓ |
|---|---|

**Language support**

**Introduction**
- *The survey at hand carried out by … and published in … focuses on/deals with …*
- *This table shows/is about/provides information about …*
- *The chart consists of …*
- *It covers the years from … to …*
- *… in percent/millimeters/kilograms/absolute numbers*

**Description**
- *Between … and …, there is an increase/decrease in …*
- *… reaches a peak/a low point in…; an all-time high*
- *The majority of … /Nearly half of …/Compared to …*
- *The chart is divided into … segments, which show …*
- *The vertical/horizontal axis represents …*
- *… is twice/three times as high as …*
- *There are more than twice as many …*
- *There are profound differences between …*
- *… drop/grow steadily/remain constant*
- *… to grow by 20% …*
- *a slight/barely noticeable rise/decrease*
- *to rank first*
- *to experience a sudden drop*
- *after a short/brief recovery*

**Interpretation/Conclusion**
- *As you can see from the diagram, …*
- *This development clearly shows/indicates that …*
- *The path of the curve reveals …*
- *The data reveals the share of …*
- *… suggests a relation between … and …*
- *So it is easy/difficult to estimate/judge/make precise comments*
- *The chart underlines the fact that …*
- *The data confirm/contradict/are not consistent with …*
- *The chart is more/less effective than … because …*
- *All in all, the statistics for … reveal/show that …*

**Language in general**
- Structure your text well and make use of paragraphs.
- Use connectives as well as phrases that are essential for this type of text.
- Vary your sentence structure.

# Cartoons

Cartoons are drawings, often either simplified or exaggerated, which comment on current topics or criticize well-known people as well as institutions in a humorous, mostly satirical way.

In order to understand a cartoon, it is essential to have a close look at its details and to pay special attention to the combination between the drawing itself and the text (e.g. caption or speech bubbles). Moreover, it is important to consider its context: Who is the cartoonist? When and where was it published? Who was it made for?

| | **Instruction: analyze, interpret** | ✓ |
|---|---|---|
| **Writing process** | **Preparation** <br> • Before you start writing, read the task carefully. <br> • Think about the cartoon – what is your first impression? What is it about? When and where was it published? <br> • Decide which elements of the cartoon are essential to understanding it. | |
| | **Introduction** <br> • Mention the name of the cartoonist and when/where the cartoon was published. <br> • Roughly outline what the cartoon depicts in general and who the target group might be. <br> • State possible reasons for the given representation. | |
| | **Description** <br> • Describe the cartoon in detail but make sure that you concentrate on the relevant aspects only. <br> • Identify the current events/people/institutions referred to. (What is being criticized?) <br> • Structure your description: Start with the most important elements in the foreground, but make sure that you do not forget those in the background. (Which details contribute to the central message of the cartoon?) <br> • If your cartoon includes text, link it to the drawing. <br> • Describe artistic techniques the cartoonist has used. (What are the methods used to portray the message?) | |
| | **Analysis/Interpretation** <br> Central question: What message is conveyed by the cartoon and how is that done? <br> • State what the cartoonist is trying to say: Use the context of the cartoon as well as the potential target audience and where it was published and interpret with these things in mind. <br> • Examine whether the issues/persons/institutions are presented in a positive or negative light and explain how this is done <br> • Pay attention to the devices used, such as the use of exaggeration, irony, puns and symbols and consider whether you can take the message at face value or not. <br> • Explain the (intended) effect on the viewer and the way it is achieved (e.g. mention pictorial elements that emphasize the message as 'proof'). <br> • Wrap up your interpretation: what is the cartoonist trying to say/criticize? | |
| | **Evaluation** <br> • Assess whether the cartoon is effective in bringing across its message. | |
| | **Editing** <br> Read through your text. Check for ... <br> • common mistakes (spelling, grammar, punctuation). <br> • variety in vocabulary used (use a dictionary for help). <br> • readability (e.g. complex sentences). <br> • repetition. <br> • a reasonable, coherent structure. | |

|  | | ✓ |
|---|---|---|
| **Language support** | **Introduction**<br>• *The cartoon by … was published in …*<br>• *The cartoon refers to …/deals with …*<br>• *The topic of the cartoon is …*<br>• *The situation reminds me of …*<br>• *My first thought when I saw the cartoon was …* | |
| | **Description**<br>• *The cartoon depicts/shows …*<br>• *In the center, there is/are*<br>• *In the background, one can see …*<br>• *… is displayed in the right-hand corner*<br>• *There is a caption at/on/in …; It says …*<br>• *The speech bubble contains …*<br>• *The cartoonist uses black-white contrast/visual metaphors to …* | |
| | **Analysis/Interpretation**<br>• *The artist is criticizing/wants to point out …*<br>• *According to the cartoonist, …*<br>• *The overall atmosphere is rather …*<br>• *The cartoon comes across as … This is achieved by the use of symbols/a pun/allusion/black humour/sarcasm …*<br>• *The characters are presented in a positive light. This is due to their facial expressions/ gestures/what they are saying.*<br>• *It is very eye-catching because of its use of …*<br>• *Although/Even though…, the real point the cartoon seems to be making is …*<br>• *The cartoonist wants to ridicule/make fun of …*<br>• *In general, the cartoonist wants to make the reader aware of …*<br>• *By presenting …, the cartoonist speaks to the viewer directly.*<br>• *The cartoon may be meant to criticize/to show …*<br>• *All in all, the cartoonist wants to make the viewer aware of the fact that …* | |
| | **Evaluation**<br>• *In my opinion, the cartoonist has successfully shown that …*<br>• *The cartoonist has failed to …*<br>• *The cartoon is (not) effective in its presentation of …*<br>• *The cartoon brings its message across convincingly/conveys its message effectively by …*<br>• *By using … the cartoonist makes this critical point clear to the viewer.* | |
| | **Language in general**<br>• Use the present progressive to describe what people are doing in the cartoon.<br>• Use the simple present when describing objects and the setting.<br>• Structure your text well and make use of paragraphs.<br>• Use connectives as well as phrases that are essential for this type of text.<br>• Vary your sentence structure. | |

# Comment

In a comment you give **your opinion** on a certain topic or statement and support your view with examples. So you have to decide what you think about the topic and why you think this. However, it may happen that you cannot reach a clear judgement on an issue. In that case, explain your views accordingly.

**Instruction:** *comment on*

| | | ✓ |
|---|---|---|
| **Writing process** | **Preparation**<br>• Before you start writing, read the task carefully.<br>• Think about your own opinion – what is your view on the issue and why do you think this?<br>• Collect and organise your thoughts/arguments and the corresponding examples. | |
| | **Introduction**<br>• Write a clear introduction in which you mention the topic/statement and explain what it means for you. If necessary, define central words/summarize the point an author makes.<br>• You can attract the reader's attention with the help of a recent event or a personal experience that illustrates the topic and/or shows its significance.<br>• Mention your attitude in the introduction if you think this attracts the reader's attention. | |
| | **Main part**<br>• Use a sentence that connects the introduction and the main part.<br>• Give arguments in favour of your personal position.<br>• Give examples (numbers, statistics, events, experts, facts etc.) to illustrate or explain your arguments.<br>• You can also mention arguments against your thesis/opinion in order to show that you are not ignoring these arguments. If you do so, you should present a strong counterargument in the same paragraph.<br>• Use one paragraph for each argument.<br>• Start each paragraph with a topic sentence which expresses what the whole paragraph is about. | |
| | **Conclusion**<br>• Briefly refer to the original question, summarize your opinion and make your point.<br>• If possible, refer to ideas mentioned in your introduction.<br>• ☞ Make sure that you do not introduce any new ideas in your conclusion. | |
| | **Editing**<br>Read through your text. Check for …<br>• common mistakes (spelling, grammar, punctuation).<br>• variety in vocabulary used (use a dictionary for help).<br>• readability (e.g. complex sentences).<br>• repetition.<br>• a reasonable, coherent structure. | |

The words below will help you to write a comment. You may add your own phrases.
Tick the phrases you have used when writing a comment yourself.

| | | ✓ |
|---|---|---|
| **Language support** | **Introduction**<br>• *The problem of … has met with a lot of attention lately …*<br>• *As far as I understand/can see …*<br>• *There are many reasons for …*<br>• *There is no doubt that …*<br>• *… claims that … . I strongly disagree with him/her.*<br>• *… claims that … . I fully agree with him / her and in this comment I will show why …* | |
| | **Main part**<br>• *In the following … I shall be concerned with …/I intend to present arguments in favour of …,*<br>• *firstly, …secondly, … another point, in addition, besides …., furthermore …, on top of that*<br>• *for example, for instance, such as, e.g.*<br>• *to illustrate this idea, I would like to …*<br>• *This idea can best be demonstrated by an example.*<br>• *There are sceptics who say … / I am fully aware that there are people who …, but … / You may have heard of people who claim …, but …*<br>• *I find it hard to believe that …* | |
| | **Conclusion**<br>• *In conclusion, I would like to say that …*<br>• *I would like to conclude by saying that …*<br>• *After having read and assessed the arguments carefully I'm sure you will agree that …*<br>• *The conclusion I draw is as follows: …*<br>• *I think it has become obvious that …* | |
| | **Language in general**<br>• Use connectives within the text (e.g. *This means that …, Thus …, As a consequence …*)<br>• Avoid imprecise and overused adjectives/adverbs (not: *good, bad, happy, sad, …*but: *convincing – positive – helpful – harmful – negative - …*)<br>• Vary your sentence structure (e.g. use participle constructions, subordinate clauses etc.) | |

# Pictures

Pictures/photos/drawings can be compared with texts. They are made with a purpose and in order to interpret what they are supposed to tell the viewer, you need a systematic approach. It is important to have a close look at its details and to consider its context (Who made it? When was it made/drawn? Where was it published? Who was it made for?) When dealing with photographs, keep in mind that there are different kinds (documentary photographs, snapshots, staged photographs). Some try to show a situation as authentically as possible, others are taken incidentally and show realistic situations without any changes whereas others were digitally altered with a special effect in mind.

**Instruction: analyze, interpret**                                                                    ✓

| Writing process | **Preparation** <br>• Before you start writing read the task carefully.<br>• Think about the picture/photo/drawing – what is your first impression? What kind of picture is it? What is it about? When and where (e.g. film, advert, internet) was it published? Who is the photographer (e.g. private person, a professional, an advertising company?) What does the title tell you?<br>• Decide which elements of the visual are essential for its understanding and note them down. | |
| --- | --- | --- |
| | **Introduction** <br>• Note down what kind of visual it is and what it shows.<br>• Mention the title, the creator's name and when/where/why it was published. | |
| | **Description** <br>• Describe the visual clearly and concentrate on the relevant aspects only.<br>• Describe in a systematic way – start with the dominant image/the main aspect and describe it in detail without forgetting the aspects in the background.<br>• If there are lots of different things in the visual or if there is no difference between foreground and background, it might be helpful to work from top to bottom, or from left to right.<br>• State where the eye is drawn to.<br>• Describe the technique the artist/painter/photographer has used. (e.g. light, colour)<br>• If there are people in the visual, describe body language and facial expressions and speculate about who the people are and what their relationship is like. | |
| | **Analysis/Interpretation** <br>Central question: What message is meant to be conveyed by the visual and how is that done?<br>• State what the artist is trying to say and how he/she does it.<br>• Speculate about the possible addressee; it might be useful to keep in mind the source of the visual (e.g. age, biased source).<br>• State whether the picture was taken with a special intention (snapshot ↔ staged photograph).<br>• If it is a staged or a manipulated photograph, assess the effect of this on the viewer.<br>• Assess how the figures are presented: in a positive, negative or neutral light? How is this done?<br>• Explain the (intended) effect on the viewer and the way it is achieved (e.g. focus, perspective, symbols).<br>• Use pictorial elements (e.g. light, colours) which underline the message as proof.<br>• Wrap up your interpretation in a final statement. | |
| | **Evaluation** <br>• Assess whether the visual is effective in bringing across its message.<br>• Outline which elements support the success/failure. | |
| | **Editing** <br>Read through your text. Check for …<br>• common mistakes (spelling, grammar, punctuation).<br>• variety in vocabulary used (use a dictionary for help).<br>    • readability (e.g. complex sentences).<br>    • repetition.<br>    • a reasonable, coherent structure. | |

**Language support**

### Introduction
- *The photo/portrait/still life/selfie/oil painting by … was published in …*
- *The picture refers to …/deals with …*
- *The topic of the photo is …*
- *The picture shows/illustrates …*
- *This is a reference to …*
- *The photo was probably taken in/at/to …*
- *The situation reminds me of …*
- *The photo is shocking/disgusting/amazing/spectacular/special…*

### Description
- *The focus of attention is on …*
- *What strikes the eye is …/the eye is drawn to …*
- *In the center, there is/are …*
- *In the foreground/background, one can see …*
- *… is displayed in the right-hand corner*
- *The artist used water colour/oil/bright colours …*
- *The photographer used black and white/colour/a sharp focus …*
- *The field size is a close-up* (very close to an object/person)/*a medium shot/a long shot* (persons/objects + surroundings)
- *to be out of focus/to be blurred*

### Analysis/Interpretation
- *The artist criticizes/wants to point out …*
- *According to the photographer, …*
- *The overall atmosphere is rather …*
- *There is a contrast between light and dark…*
- *The photo comes across as …. This is achieved by …*
- *The characters are presented in a positive light. This is due to their facial expressions/ gestures/what they are saying.*
- *X seems to be sad/distracted/angry/embarrassed … because …*
- *From the people's looks, I can assume that …*
- *The colours support the impression that … The light/the colours create/contribute to …*
- *The photo is a good example of …*
- *In general, the artist wants to make the viewer aware of …*
- *The photo is meant to criticize …*

### Evaluation
- *Personally, I do/do not like the photo, because …. The photo impresses me/does not impress me because …*
- *My initial reaction to the picture was …, but on second glance I think that …*
- *In my opinion, the artist has successfully shown that …*
- *The picture does not reach the intended target group because ….*
- *The photo is (not) effective in its presentation of …*
- *It could have been more effective if it had …*

### Language in general
- Use the present progressive to describe what people are doing in the visual.
- Use the simple present when describing objects and the setting.
- Structure your text well and make use of paragraphs.
- Use connectives as well as phrases that are essential for this type of text.
- Vary your sentence structure.

# Argumentative Essay

In an argumentative essay, you **discuss** a topic or statement by presenting different positions or points of view. After having read your essay, the reader should be aware that there are different ways of looking at the given topic or statement. Even though you have to stay neutral when weighing up different sides of an issue in the main part of your essay, it is possible to give your own opinion or simply appeal to the reader to draw their own conclusion in the concluding paragraph.

The structure of your argumentative essay can vary, depending on the topic or statement that you write about. The following two patterns are the most common:

| Pattern 1 |
|---|
| Introduction |
| 1. Arguments +    2. Arguments − |
| Conclusion |

| Pattern 2 |
|---|
| Introduction |
| Argument + → Argument − |
| → Argument + → Argument − |
| → Argument + → Argument − |
| Conclusion |

**Instruction: discuss** ✓

| Writing process | | |
|---|---|---|
| | **Preparation**<br>• Before you start writing, read the task carefully.<br>• Then brainstorm ideas on a sheet of paper, collect arguments and corresponding examples for the different positions.<br>• Then decide on the structure of your essay and the sequence of the arguments. | |
| | **Introduction**<br>• Write a clear, thought-provoking introduction, in which you present your issue/statement and show why it is important to discuss this issue.<br>• Attract the reader's attention for example with the help of a recent event, or a personal experience, a reference to a famous person. | |
| | **Main part**<br>• Use a sentence that connects the introduction and the main part.<br>• Present the different positions/points of view and the corresponding arguments.<br>• Provide examples for each position/point of view/argument (facts, statistics etc.).<br>• Use one paragraph for each single position/point of view/argument.<br>• Start each paragraph with a topic sentence, expressing what the whole paragraph is about.<br>• If possible, finish with the argument that you find most convincing.<br>• ☞ Do not express your own position in the main part of your essay but only present the various positions/points of view/arguments. | |
| | **Conclusion**<br>• Briefly refer to the original question and wrap up the discussion.<br>• Give your final position on the topic (this can be a compromise) without repeating your arguments or leave it to the reader to draw their own conclusion.<br>• If possible, refer to the event or personal experience you have mentioned in the beginning or speculate about the significance of the topic/statement in the near future.<br>• ☞ Make sure that you do not introduce any new ideas in your conclusion. | |
| | **Editing**<br>Read through your text. Check for …<br>• common mistakes (spelling, grammar, punctuation).<br>• variety in vocabulary used (use a dictionary for help).<br>• readability (e.g. complex sentences).<br>• repetition.<br>• a reasonable, coherent structure. | |

The words in the box help will you to write a comment. You may add your own phrases. Tick the phrases you have used when writing an argumentative essay yourself.

| | ✓ |
|---|---|

**Language support**

### Introduction

- *In this essay, I want to investigate…/This essay will concentrate on …/My discussion draws into focus …*
- *… seems to be an inexhaustible source of controversy/… is a hotly debated topic at the moment/The problem of … has been met with a lot of attention lately*
- *It is interesting to weigh up the benefits and drawbacks of …*
- *Therefore, one should discuss the issue …/wonder about/ask the question of whether …*

### Description

- *In the following … I shall be concerned with …/I intend to present arguments in favour of …*
- *some experts state that …/many people believe/claim that …*
- *firstly, …secondly, …/another point/in addition/besides/furthermore/on top of that*
- *for example/for instance/such as/e.g.*
- *To illustrate this idea, I would like to …/This idea can best be demonstrated by an example.*
- *however/although/whereas/in spite of*
- *It raises questions about …*
- *… could lead to/cause …*
- *It is true that …. but …*
- *One reason for criticism is that …, yet …*

### Conclusion

- *All in all, it can be said that …/In conclusion, I would like to say that … /, I would like to conclude by saying that …/After weighing up the arguments carefully …/The conclusion I draw is as follows: …*
- *as a consequence …/as a result of …/therefore, …*
- *The most important aspect one has to keep in mind is …*
- *After all …, there can be no doubt as regards …*
- *I am absolutely convinced of …/In my opinion …*
- *apparently/obviously*
- *to my mind…/I firmly believe that …*
- *to a certain extent, I can accept …., but…/although …, we must admit that …*

### Language in general

- Use neutral language (☞ do not use "I think" in the main part of the essay).
- Use connectives within the text.
- Avoid imprecise and overused adjectives/adverbs.
- Vary your sentence structure. (e.g. use participle constructions, subordinate clauses etc.)

# Basic Operators

In the following you will find a list of frequently used operators. The list includes the operators as well as explanations and examples.

| Operator | Explanation | Example |
|---|---|---|
| analyze | describe and explain in detail | Analyze the way(s) in which atmosphere is created. |
| assess | express a well-founded opinion on the nature or quality of sb./sth. | Assess the importance of learning languages for somebody's future. |
| evaluate | express a well-founded opinion on the nature or quality of sb./sth. | Evaluate the success of the steps taken so far to reduce pollution. |
| examine | describe and explain in detail | Examine the opposing views on social class held by the two protagonists. |
| give/write a characterization of | provide a thorough analysis of a character | Give a characterization of the protagonist in the excerpt. |
| comment (on) | state one's opinion clearly and support one's view with evidence or reasons | Comment on the writer's view on gender roles. |
| compare | show similarities and differences | Compare the opinions on education held by the experts presented in the text. |
| describe | give a detailed account of what sb./sth. is like | Describe the soldier's outward appearance. |
| discuss | give arguments or reasons for and against, especially to come to a well-founded conclusion | Discuss whether social status determines somebody's future options. |
| explain | make sth. clear | Explain the protagonist's obsession with money. |
| illustrate | use examples to explain or make clear | Illustrate the way in which school life in Britain differs from that in Germany. |
| interpret | explain the meaning or purpose of sth. | Interpret the message of the cartoon. |
| outline | give the main features, structure or general principles of sth. | Outline the writer's views on love, marriage and divorce. |
| point out | present the main aspects of sth. briefly and clearly | Point out the author's ideas on… |
| state | present the main aspects of sth. briefly and clearly | State your reasons for applying for a high school year. |
| Summarize/sum up | give a concise account of the main points or ideas of a text, issue or topic | Summarize the text. Sum up the information given about green energy. |
| Write (+ text type) | produce a text with specific features | Write the ending of the story/a letter to the editor/a dialogue etc. |

*(Selection is based on https://www.iqb.hu-berlin.de/abitur/dokumente/englisch and https://rp.baden-wuerttemberg.de/rpt/Abt7/Fachberater/Documents/rpt-75-fsp-servicepaket_neu_12-02-2013.pdf)*

| English word | German equivalent | additional ... |
|---|---|---|

## Chapter 1 – The Ambiguity of Belonging

| English word | German equivalent | additional ... |
|---|---|---|
| belonging | *Zugehörigkeitsgefühl* | to create a sense of belonging, lack of belonging, to belong to; Do you belong here? |
| autonomy | *Autonomie, Unabhängigkeit* | individual/personal/financial autonomy, to enjoy/have/gain/seek/struggle for/grant autonomy (from) |
| relatedness | *Beziehung, Verwandtschaft, Verbundenheit* | relate to God |
| failure | *Misserfolg, Versagen, Scheitern* | to be a failure, to admit failure, fear of failure, to fail |
| isolation | *Isolation, Absonderung, Entkopplung, Abgeschiedenheit* | enforced isolation, to suffer from/experience isolation, to isolate oneself from, splendid isolation |
| basic needs | *Grundbedürfnisse* | to fulfill needs, needs are met, to feel needed |
| social ties/bonds | *Soziale Bindungen* | to easily form/strengthen/maintain social ties |
| relationships | *Beziehungen* | to maintain/build up/establish/break off relationships, to relate to, healthy/strong/broken/fragile/troubled/close/intimate/lasting relationships |
| attachments | *Bindungen* | enduring interpersonal attachments, develop/have/form a feeling of social attachment, close/deep/passionate attachments |
| to be sure | *sich sicher sein/überzeugt sein* | to be sure of oneself |
| to feel safe | *sich sicher fühlen* | safety net |
| to feel secure | *sich sicher/geborgen fühlen* | security, a safe haven of comfort and security |
| to cause pain | *Schmerz verursachen* | to result in pain, to be painful, unbearable/agonizing pain, to be in pain |
| identity | *Identität, Persönlichkeit* | to identify with, identity card, identity theft, to disclose one's identity, true/false/cultural/assumed identity, to change/discover/establish one's identity |
| alienation | *Entfremdung* | to feel alienated from, growing alienation from |
| difference | *Unterschied* | to differ from, significant/crucial/essential difference, the difference lies in, this makes all the difference |
| identification | *Identifikation* | to identify with |
| inclusion | *Inklusion, Einschluss, Einbeziehung* | to include somebody, opposite: exclusion |
| loneliness | *Einsamkeit* | to be lonely, to suffer from aching/terrible loneliness |
| to feel ambivalent | *zwiegespalten sein* | to feel two ways about the relationship |
| ambiguous | *mehrdeutig sein* | The ending of the novel is ambiguous. |
| personality traits | *Charaktereigenschaften* | to have appealing/negative/distinctive character traits, to display certain character traits |
| selfhood | *Individualität, Persönlichkeit* | Being happy is the hallmark of good selfhood. |
| affinity | *Affinität, Seelenverwandschaft* | to show/display natural/close affinity for (things)/towards (human beings) |
| to lean on sb. | *sich auf jemanden verlassen* | She leans on him. |
| kinship | *(Seelen-)Verwandtschaft* | ties of kinship |
| loyalty | *Loyalität, Treue* | to be loyal to, to show loyalty, to win/expect loyalty |
| acceptance | *Akzeptanz, Anerkennung* | to find/win/gain acceptance |
| to be uncertain | *sich nicht sicher sein* | uncertain times, life is uncertain |
| doubt | *Zweifel* | to doubt, to raise doubts, to be in doubt, beyond doubt |

| English word | German equivalent | additional ... |
|---|---|---|

## Chapter 2 – The Child

| English word | German equivalent | additional ... |
|---|---|---|
| to stagger | schwanken/taumeln | → He staggered off into the night. |
| to slap sb. | jdn. schlagen (ins Gesicht) | to slap sb. in the face, to slap hands |
| to yell | schreien/brüllen | to yell across , to yell out, to yell with fear |
| to strut | stolzieren | to strut along, to strut past |
| to disgrace sb. | Schande über jdn/etw bringen | to be a disgrace to sb., to bring disgrace on |
| to smooth | glätten | → smooth faced |
| due | fällig | past due, when due, sth. is due |
| coach | Waggon | coach driver |
| to be passed out | ohnmächtig | to be passed out drunk |
| to gaze | anstarren/nachschauen | to gaze after sb., gaze at sb. |
| envious | neidisch / missgünstig | to be envious, envious person |
| to recommend | empfehlen / vorschlagen | to fully recommend, to recommend against |
| suspense | Spannung, Ungewissheit | to keep sb. in suspense, agony of suspense, arc of suspense |
| ambitious | ehrgeizig | ambitious aims, ambitious dream, ambitious of |
| determined | entschlossen | determined to continue, I am detemined not to waste my time |
| furious | wütend | to become furious (about sth.), to be visibly furious |
| neglected | vernachlässigt | in a neglected condition, poverty-related and neglected diseases |
| sensitive | sensibel | a highly sensitive, caring man, to be acutely/highly/painfully/very sensitive |

## Chapter 3 – Gran Torino

| English word | German equivalent | additional ... |
|---|---|---|
| run-down | baufällig, verlottert | a run-down building |
| standard of living | Lebensstandard | Many people in Western Europe enjoy a high standard of living. |
| prosperity | Wohlstand | → prosperous, the prosperous middle-class |
| decline | Niedergang | This building symbolizes the decline of Detroit. |
| to abandon | verlassen, aufgeben | He was abandoned by her. |
| to be employed | angestellt sein | Many American workers used to be employed in the auto industry. |
| assembly line | Fließband | to work on an assembly line |
| bankrupt | bankrott | to go bankrupt, → bankruptcy |
| peak | Gipfel | At the age of 45, he was at the peak of his career. |
| the needy | die Bedürftigen | The needy are provided for by organizations such as the Red Cross. |
| available | verfügbar, vorhanden | Because there are not enough jobs available in Detroit, unemployment is high. |
| unemployment | Arbeitslosigkeit | → to be unemployed |
| foreclosure | Zwangsvollstreckung | A considerable number of Americans are threatened by foreclosure. |
| recession | Abschwung, Rezession | Detroit has been heavily affected by the economic recession. |
| suburb | Vorstadt | → to live in suburban America, the prosperous suburbs of Detroit |
| to persuade sb. | jdn. überreden | → to be persuasive, the art of persuasion |

| English word | German equivalent | additional ... |
|---|---|---|
| disappointed | *enttäuscht* | → disappointment; to be utterly disappointed |
| grumpy | *mürrisch* | a grumpy, old man |
| dutiful | *pflichtbewusst* | → She considers it her duty to take care of the unemployed. |
| hypocritical | *heuchlerisch* | → to be a hypocrite |
| spoiled | *verwöhnt* | Ashley comes across as a spoiled teenager who doesn't know how to behave appropriately. |
| rude | *derb, grob* | rude behaviour, to make a rude comment |
| outward appearance | *Aussehen, Erscheinungsbild* | His outward appearance attracted attention. |
| to rebel against sth. | *gegen etw. rebellieren* | → to be a rebel |
| predominantly | *vorwiegend, überwiegend* | an area predominantly inhabited by whites, the predominant color is grey |
| impression | *Eindruck* | to make a good/profound/lasting impression, he had the impression that she … |
| disgusted | *angewidert* | → feelings of disgust, to cause disgust |
| pity | *Mitleid* | to feel pity for sb., → to pity sb. |
| pressure | *Druck* | → to be pressured by sb. |
| relieved | *erleichtert* | → He felt such relief when he shared his worries with him., the relief of pain |
| burden | *Last* | → He had always been burdened by these experiences. |
| to admit | *zugeben* | to admit your guilt |
| to convey | *vermitteln, transportieren* | to convey an image, to convey information to sb., to convey a message/impression/idea |
| reluctant | *zurückhaltend* | → to show considerable reluctance |
| considerate | *rücksichtsvoll* | a kind and considerate man |
| determined | *entschlossen* | → to show great determination |
| self-reliant | *selbständig* | He wanted his sons to become self-reliant. |
| content | *zufrieden* | She was content with his work. |
| to praise sb. | *jdn. loben* | He hardly ever praised his employees even though they usually did a good job. |
| relationship | *Beziehung* | to have a close/intimate/complex/loving/professional/strained relationship |
| awkward | *hilflos, unbehaglich* | an awkward situation, to feel awkward |
| custom | *Gewohnheit, Brauch* | It is our custom to visit relatives on Sundays. He was unfamiliar with local customs. |
| development | *Entwicklung* | to undergo a development, this development was affected by … |
| guidance | *Führung, Anleitung* | to offer guidance, to provide guidance |
| to coerce sb. | *jdn. nötigen, jdn. zwingen* | to coerce sb. into doing sth., → without any coercion |
| to complain | *sich beklagen* | → no cause for complaint |

| English word | German equivalent | additional ... |
|---|---|---|

## Chapter 4.1 – Family and Friends

| **Section A** | | |
|---|---|---|
| nuclear family | *Kernfamilie* | the nuclear family as the traditional paradigm family |
| extended family | *Großfamilie* | Single-parent families as well as extended or blended families are a sign of diverse family structures. |
| single-parent | *Alleinerziehende(r)* | |
| blended family | *Patchworkfamilie* | |
| kinship | *(Bluts-)Verwandtschaft* | The ties of kinship are often strong. |
| → voluntary kin | *freiwillige Verwandtschaft* | Godparents are a good example of voluntary kinship. |
| to cohabit | *zusammenleben (nicht verh.)* | |
| divorce | *Scheidung* | to file for divorce → to divorce sb., to separate from sb. |
| to separate | *sich trennen* | → to go separate ways |
| estranged | *zerstritten, entfremdet* | Coping with estranged parents can be difficult. |
| to (re-)marry | *(wieder)heiraten* | → married/unmarried/remarried |
| (non-)marital | *(nicht) ehelich* | to have marital problems |
| stepfather/-mother/-sister ... | *Stiefvater/-mutter...* | |
| half-brother/-sister | *Halbbruder/-schwester* | |
| offspring | *Nachwuchs, Nachkomme* | problems with teenage offspring |
| siblings | *Geschwister* | sibling rivalry |
| an only child | *ein Einzelkind* | |
| incarcerated | *inhaftiert* | children of incarcerated fathers |
| household chores | *Hausarbeit* | to share/help with household chores |
| adolescence | *Jugendalter* | in early/late adolescence; → an adolescent (*ein Jugendlicher*) |
| adult | *Erwachsener* | to spend one's entire adult life |
| peer | *Gleichaltrige* | |
| friend | *Freund* | a best/close/closest/dear/lifelong/trusted friend |
| to be related to one another | *miteinander verwandt sein* | |
| to be met with more easily | *etwas einfacher bewältigen können* | |
| a generally accepted ideal | *ein allgemein anerkanntes Ideal* | |
| to be less likely to | *weniger wahrscheinlich sein* | Black children are less likely to live in two-parent households. |
| unconditional love | *bedingungslose Liebe* | Many parents show unconditional love for their children. |
| It runs in the family. | *Es liegt in der Familie.* | |
| **Section B** | | |
| relationship | *Beziehung* | to end/maintain/establish/break off/build up a relationship, a stable/close/intimate/strained/superficial/beneficial/close-knit relationship |
| distance | *Distanz* | to bridge/widen the distance, → to distance oneself from, → to keep one's distance |
| gap | *Kluft* | to widen/bridge the gap |
| alienation | *Entfremdung* | a growing alienation from sb., a sense of alienation, → to feel alienated from sb. |

| English word | German equivalent | additional ... |
|---|---|---|
| bond | *Bindung* | familial bonds, to develop a bond with sb. |
| connection | *Verbindung* | a strong connection between<br>→ to feel closely connected to sb. |
| → connections | *entfernte Verwandte* | |
| pressure | *Druck* | to put pressure on sb. |
| solitude | *Einsamkeit* | to seek/avoid solitude |
| solace | *Trost* | to give/seek solace |
| comfort | *Trost* | to take comfort in sth. |
| affiliation | *Zugehörigkeit* | a need for affiliation, family affiliation |
| responsibility | *Verantwortung* | to accept/assume/take responsibility |
| well-being | *Wohlergehen* | to contribute to the emotional/mental well-being |
| resilience | *Widerstandsfähigkeit* | to show a remarkable resilience to sth. |
| to provide | *bereitstellen* | to provide stability/a sense of belonging |
| to rely on sb. | *sich auf jdn. verlassen* | |
| to share secrets with sb. | *Geheimnisse mit jdm. teilen* | |
| to be fond of sb. | *jdn. mögen* | |
| to lose touch with sb. | *den Kontakt zu jdm. verlieren* | |
| to have a lot in common with sb. | *viel mit jdm. gemeinsam haben* | |
| to feel safe/ appreciated | *sich sicher/gewertschätzt fühlen* | |
| to be lied to | *angelogen werden* | |
| **Section C** | | |
| company | *Begleitung* | to enjoy sb.'s company<br>to keep sb. company |
| trust | *Vertrauen* | mutual trust, a lack of trust destroys relationships,<br>→ to trust sb.<br>→ trustworthy: You can rely on him. He is trustworthy. |
| loyalty | *Loyalität* | loyalty to/towards sb., to count on sb.'s loyalty,<br>→ to stay loyal to sb. |
| protection | *Schutz* | protection of sb. against/from sth.,<br>→ to protect sb. from |
| to feel kinship with sb. | *sich jdm. verwandt fühlen* | |
| to humiliate | *erniedrigen* | to feel humiliated by sb. |
| to be possessive/ bossy | *vereinnahmend/herrisch* | He seems intensely possessive to me. |
| to be assertive | *bestimmt sein* | Try to be more assertive so that people take notice. |
| to be submissive/ obedient | *unterwürfig/gehorsam sein* | → unquestioning obedience |

| English word | German equivalent | additional ... |
|---|---|---|

## Chapter 4.2 – The American Dream

| | | |
|---|---|---|
| **Section A** | | |
| opportunity | *Möglichkeit, Chance* | to be guaranteed equal/unlimited opportunities |
| prosperity | *Wohlstand* | → to prosper, the promise of prosperity, the opportunity to prosper and succeed |
| persecution | *Verfolgung* | to suffer from religious persecution; → to be persecuted |
| poverty | *Armut* | to live in poverty, a poverty-stricken area, to live below the poverty line, to reduce poverty |
| to achieve | *erreichen* | to achieve an aim, → a major achievement |
| to come true | *wahr werden* | to make a dream come true |
| to discriminate against so | *jdn diskrimieren* | Some of the immigrants were discriminated against in their home countries. |
| transformation | *Verwandlung* | the narrative of a transformation |
| conviction | *Überzeugung* | the conviction that everyone has equal chances, → to be convinced that ... |
| self-determination | *Selbstbestimmung* | to live a self-determined life |
| immigration wave | *Einwanderungswelle* | Many immigration waves were caused by wars or famines. |
| rag | *Lumpen* | from rags to riches |
| controversial | *kontrovers* | a controversial topic |
| aspiration | *Anspruch, Streben* | to have high aspirations |
| claim | *Behauptung, Anspruch* | → the author claims that ..., the claim that life was better and richer and fuller ... |
| to establish | *aufbauen, errichten* | to establish an ideal society |
| to participate | *teilnehmen, teilhaben* | → participation, to participate in politics |
| ability | *Fähigkeit* | to live up to one's abilities, the ability to read and write |
| circumstances | *Umstände* | favourable economic circumstances |
| fortune | *Vermögen* | to make a fortune |
| welfare | *Sozialhilfe* | to live on welfare |
| gap | *Kluft, Lücke* | the gap between the rich and the poor |
| issue | *Thema, Angelegenheit* | the issue of racism, to discuss an issue |
| to sacrifice sth. | *etw. opfern* | He would never sacrifice his principles. |
| **Section B** | | |
| to share | *teilen, gemeinsam haben* | to share values, to share the profits, to share a room, to share convictions |
| division | *Spaltung, Teilung* | to be divided into |
| to take advantage of sth. | *einen Nutzen ziehen aus, ausnutzen* | to take advantage of an opportunity, to take advantage of sb.'s weaknesses |
| to be able to afford | *es sich leisten können* | Many Americans aren't able to afford proper health insurance. |
| to make a living | *seinen Lebensunterhalt verdienen* | She was struggling to make a living as an artist. |
| to raise a family | *Kinder aufziehen, eine Familie gründen* | to start a family, to raise children |
| to share sth. | *etwas gemeinsam haben, etw. teilen* | to share a room, to share memories, to share the same values |
| to consist of | *bestehen aus, zusammengesetzt sein aus* | to consist of various elements, to be made up of |

| English word | German equivalent | additional ... |
|---|---|---|
| **Section C** | | |
| urban / rural | *städtisch / ländlich* | an urban setting, a rural upbringing |
| run-down | *heruntergekommen* | a run-down building, a run-down business |
| in good shape | *in gutem Zustand* | to keep sth. in good shape |
| to neglect sth. | *vernachlässigen* | → a neglected area, a neglected school |
| to look down on sb. | *auf jdn. herabblicken* | There are still people in the South who look down on African Americans. |
| porch | *Veranda* | to sit on the front porch |
| apprentice | *Lehrling* | → to do an apprenticeship |
| to feel ambivalent about | *gespaltene Gefühle haben* | → ambivalence, to feel ambivalent about immigration |
| to instill pride in sb. | *jdn. mit Stolz erfüllen* | His work has always instilled pride in him. |
| considerable | *erheblich, beträchtlich* | to have a considerable influence on sb., to require a considerable effort |
| attainable | *erreichbar* | an attainable goal, an attainable objective |

# Chapter 4.3 – Immigration

| Section A | | |
|---|---|---|
| country of origin | *Herkunftsland* | Mexico is her country of origin. |
| destination | *Ziel, Bestimmungsort* | Germany is one of the top destinations of many migrants. |
| persecution | *Verfolgung* | → to be persecuted because of religious reasons |
| immigration | *Einwanderung* | first-generation immigrant, as a consequence of mass immigration, immigration wave |
| lure | *Verlockung, Reiz* | the lure of a better life |
| refugee | *Flüchtling* | refugee camp, → to seek refuge from … |
| border control | *Grenzkontrolle* | to strengthen border control |
| asylum seeker | *Asylsuchende(r)* | → to seek asylum, to be granted asylum |
| resident | *Bewohner* | to be a permanent resident of … |
| naturalization | *Einbürgerung* | → to be a naturalized citizen, to hope for naturalization |
| oppression | *Unterdrückung* | to suffer from oppression, → to be oppressed |
| to increase | *ansteigen* | … the number of immigrants increased in the … |
| comparatively | *vergleichsweise* | comparatively few immigrants came in … |
| decline | *Rückgang* | to witness a decline, → … the number declined due to … |
| influx | *Zustrom* | an influx of immigrants |
| to escape | *fliehen, entkommen* | to escape oppression/persecution |
| improvement | *Verbesserung* | → to improve your living conditions, to be a major improvement |
| prospect | *Aussicht* | the prospect of a better life / higher status |
| to encourage | *ermutigen, fördern* | the claim that lax immigration laws encourage immigration |
| threat | *Bedrohung* | to pose a threat, to be regarded as a threat, → threatening, to threaten |
| to exaggerate | *übertreiben* | → exaggeration, the threat was grossly exaggerated |
| poverty | *Armut* | to flee from poverty, to live in poverty |
| to take advantage of sth. | *etw. ausnutzen* | to take advantage of the welfare system |
| welfare | *Sozialhilfe* | to live on welfare, to be granted welfare benefits |

| English word | German equivalent | additional ... |
|---|---|---|
| undocumented | *ohne Papiere* | undocumented workers |
| survey | *Umfrage* | to conduct a survey, according to a survey |
| to outperform | *übertreffen* | second-generation immigrants often outperform their parents in terms of … |
| assimilation | *Anpassung* | → to be fully assimilated |
| estimation | *Schätzung* | → it is estimated that … |
| integration | *Integration* | → to be integrated, the integration of immigrants is a major challenge for countries such as … |
| to merge | *verschmelzen* | … quickly merged with the local population |
| **Section B** | | |
| appropriate | *passend, angemessen* | She didn't behave appropriately when she …, His remark was an appropriate response. |
| finding | *Befund, Erkenntnis* | The findings of the survey indicate that … |
| scientific | *wissenschaftlich* | → to work in science, to be a scientist |
| pledge of allegiance | *Treueschwur* | Most American students recite the pledge of allegiance every day at school. |
| notion | *Idee, Vorstellung* | a misguided notion |
| to be met with open arms | *mit offenen Armen empfangen werden* | She was met with open arms by her family when returning from prison. |
| abroad | *im Ausland* | to live abroad, to spend time abroad |
| to take into consideration | *berücksichtigen* | We must take into consideration that he lived abroad for ten years. |
| stranger | *Fremder* | to feel like a stranger in one's own country |
| to be familiar with | *mit etw. vertraut sein* | to be familiar with traditions and customs |
| to assess | *beurteilen, bewerten* | It is difficult to assess whether illegal immigration has a positive or negative effect on the country's economy. |
| to approve of sth. | *etw. gutheißen, etw. befürworten* | She doesn't approve of his immigration policy. |
| to prevent | *verhindern, unterbinden* | … disapproved of his idea that the USA should prevent Muslims from entering the country. |
| **Section C** | | |
| rural | *ländlich* | a rural area; … is typical of rural America |
| to remain | *bleiben, zurückbleiben* | to remain seated, … has to remain in hospital for two more weeks. |
| lack | *Mangel* | a lack of opportunities |
| root | *Wurzel* | → Obama claimed racism was deeply rooted in society. |
| minority | *Minderheit* | Immigrants from Europe are in the minority in … |
| ancestor | *Vorfahre* | His ancestors came from Norway. |
| reputation | *Ruf, Ansehen* | Her reputation has been damaged by the … |
| affluent | *wohlhabend, begütert* | → The country's affluence has lured immigrants for hundreds of years. |
| upward mobility | *sozialer Aufstieg* | a lack of opportunities for upward mobility |
| threat | *Bedrohung* | → threatening, to pose a threat to … |
| decline | *Niedergang* | the decline of the auto industry in Detroit |
| bond | *Verbundenheit* | to maintain strong bonds |
| sentiment | *Empfindung, Meinung* | an increase in racist sentiments |
| priority | *Vorrang* | In Hmong culture, the family takes priority and individual needs … |
| to display | *zeigen, ausstellen* | → to be on display |

| English word | German equivalent | additional ... |
|---|---|---|

## Chapter 4.4 – Race

| | | |
|---|---|---|
| **Section A** | | |
| race | *Rasse* | race relations, → racial equality, racial profiling |
| inferior/superior | *unterlegen/überlegen* | to be regarded as inferior, to feel superior, → a feeling of superiority, inferiority complex |
| to humiliate sb. | *jdn. erniedrigen* | → humiliation, to be humiliated |
| ethnicity | *Ethnie, Volkszugehörigkeit* | → ethnic diversity, ethnic minority |
| dominance | *Überlegenheit, Vorherrschaft* | → to be dominant, white dominance |
| to discriminate against sb. | *jdn. diskriminieren* | to be discriminated against, → to suffer from discrimination |
| to exploit | *ausbeuten* | → exploitation, to be exploited |
| segregation | *Rassentrennung* | racial segregation, the end of segregation → segregated schools |
| to legitimize | *legitimieren, rechtfertigen* | to legitimize slavery, → a legitimate concern |
| to deny | *aberkennen, leugnen* | to be denied basic rights |
| widespread | *weitverbreitet* | racism was widespread in the South |
| inequality | *Ungleichheit* | social inequality, → an unequal distribution of wealth |
| contempt | *Verachtung* | to be met with contempt, to feel contempt for ... |
| disadvantage | *Nachteil, Benachteiligung* | → to be disadvantaged, to suffer from disadvantages |
| attainment | *Leistung, Errungenschaft* | educational attainment, → to attain your full potential |
| exclusion | *Ausschluss, Ausgrenzung* | → African-Americans were excluded from power The exclusion of ethnic minorities. |
| to earn a degree | *einen Abschluss machen* | to earn a college degree |
| **Section B** | | |
| stereotype | *Klischee* | a popular stereotype, → to be stereotyped |
| minority | *Minderheit* | to be in the minority, ethnic minority |
| prejudice | *Vorurteil* | → to be prejudiced against, his actions were motivated by prejudice |
| to distinguish | *unterscheiden, auseinanderhalten* | to distinguish between two kinds of ..., |
| features | *Eigenschaften, Charakterzüge* | to assign features or characteristics to people |
| to categorize | *kategorisieren* | People tend to categorize other people on the basis of external features. |
| to benefit from | *profitieren von* | The country has always benefited from its favorable location. |
| to offend so. | *jdn. verletzen* | → offensive language, to be offended by a remark |
| stigma | *Makel, Brandmal* | → to be stigmatized, the stigma of being an ex-prisoner |
| intention | *Absicht* | to have good intentions, → to intend to do sth. |
| to favor | *favorisieren, bevorzugen* | This tax policy favors the wealthy. |
| **Section C** | | |
| perception | *Wahrnehmung, Sichtweise* | → She was perceived as African American, even though ... |
| to affect | *betreffen, beeinflussen* | African Americans were adversely affected by segregation. |
| to mingle | *(sich) mischen* | → racial mingling, at school she mingled with students from different races. |
| self-confidence | *Selbstbewusstsein* | → to be self-confident, to lack self-confidence |
| to assign | *zuordnen* | to assign certain characteristics or features to people |

| English word | German equivalent | additional ... |
|---|---|---|
| barbarian | *barbarisch* | uncivilized, primitive |
| civilized | *zivilisiert* | civilized behaviour, a civilized society |
| to draw a conclusion | *einen Schluss ziehen* | Which conclusions can you draw from your findings? |
| to depict | *zeigen, abbilden* | Are the Hmong depicted as barbarian in *Gran Torino*? |

## Chapter 4.5 – Gun Culture

| Section A | | |
|---|---|---|
| (fire)arms | *(Schuss)Waffen* | to carry firearms, the right to bear arms, → to be (un)armed |
| militia | *Miliz, Bürgerwehr* | to serve in a militia, to be a member of a militia |
| to be familiar with | *vertraut sein mit* | to be familiar with weapons |
| gun owner | *Waffenbesitzer* | the number of gun owners is higher in ... → privately owned guns |
| opponent | *Gegner* | → to oppose, opposition<br>There are many people who oppose gun ownership. |
| self-defense | *Selbstverteidigung* | to act in self-defense |
| gun show | *Waffenmesse* | to visit a gun show |
| shooting range | *Schießstand* | a place where people practise shooting on targets |
| amendment | *Verfassungszusatz* | Gun ownership is guaranteed by the Second Amendment. |
| proponent | *Befürworter* | proponents of gun ownership |
| advocate | *Fürsprecher* | He's a fervent advocate of strict gun control. |
| issue | *Thema, Problem* | a controversial issue |
| to be fascinated by | *fasziniert sein von* | → fascination; Guns have always held a fascination for her. |
| independence | *Unabhängigkeit, Selbständigkeit* | → to be/feel independent, a symbol of independence |
| to survive | *überleben* | → survival, to be essential for survival |
| upbringing | *Erziehung* | a religious upbringing, a strict upbringing |
| to introduce a law | *ein Gesetz einführen* | to introduce stricter gun laws |
| to restrict | *einschränken* | to restrict the access to guns |
| to prevent | *verhindern* | to prevent a crime by ... |
| national identity | *nationales Selbstverständnis* | to be part of America's national identity |
| rifle | *Gewehr, Büchse* | NRA = National Rifle Association (an organization which advocates for gun rights and an influential lobbying group) |
| Section B | | |
| to hunt | *jagen* | → hunter, hunting is a popular pastime among ... to be good at hunting |
| woods | *Wald* | to live in the woods |
| to aim at sth. | *auf etw. zielen* | He aimed at the deer but missed it. |
| to fit in | *sich anpassen* | She had problems fitting in because ... |
| deer | *Hirsch* | to go deer hunting |
| approval | *Anerkennung, Akzeptanz* | He experienced a level of approval he had never experienced before. |
| extraordinary | *außergewöhnlich* | Her achievements were extraordinary. |
| to prefer sth. | *etw. bevorzugen* | Do your prefer coffee or tea? |
| to feel miserable | *sich elend fühlen* | She felt miserable after eating five pieces of ... |

| English word | German equivalent | additional ... |
|---|---|---|
| **Section C** | | |
| sense of security | *Gefühl von Sicherheit* | It gave him a sense of security. |
| pastime | *Zeitvertreib* | His favorite pastimes were shooting and golf. |
| masculine | *männlich* | → masculinity, to assume masculine ways |
| tool | *Werkzeug* | Guns are essential tools for hunting. |
| to cause harm | *Schaden zufügen* | … has the potential to cause great harm. |
| ambivalent | *zwiespältig* | to have an ambivalent relationship with |
| to impress sb. | *jdn. beeindrucken* | He was impressed by his … |
| to threaten sb. | *jdn. bedrohen* | to threaten somebody with a gun |
| to haunt sb. | *jdn. heimsuchen, verfolgen* | He is haunted by his past. |
| to pull the trigger | *den Abzug betätigen* | When you pull the trigger, the bullet is fired. |
| atrocity | *Gräueltat* | to commit atrocities |
| to order sb. to do sth. | *jdm. eine Anweisung erteilen etw. zu tun* | He was ordered to surrender. |
| to trust sb. | *jdm. vertrauen* | Priests are trusted by many people. |
| to bless sb. | *jdn. segnen* | He blessed the couple, then they were married. |
| mercy | *Gnade* | to beg for mercy, → merciful, merciless, to have mercy on sb. |
| role model | *Vorbild* | to serve as a role model |

## Bildquellenverzeichnis

## Textquellenverzeichnis

| | |
|---|---|
| 14-16 | "The Child" by Julius Lester, in: Donald R. Gallo (Ed.), Join In: Multiethnic Short Stories by Outstanding Writers for Young Adults, Laurel Leaf Books 1995. |
| 24 | "Do White Males Feel They Are Losing Their "Space?" by Rosalind C. Barnett, Ph.D., and Caryl Rivers on www.psychologytoday.com, 4 January 2019. |
| 50 | "The Epic of America" by James Truslow Adams, Blue Ribbon Books, 1931. |
| 50 | "Reinventing the American Dream" by Alondra Alba on www.theodysseyonline.com, 14 December 2015. |
| 50 | "Hillbilly Elegy: A Memoir of a Family and Culture in Crisis" by J.D. Vance, Harper, 2016. |
| 50 | "Outside coastal cities an 'other America' has different values and challenges" by Chris Arnade on www.theguardian.com, 21 February 2017. |
| 55 | Speech by Barack Obama, held in Bettendorf, Iowa, 7 November 2007. |
| 62 | "The New Colossus" by Emma Lazarus, Liberty State Park. |
| 68-69 | "My least favourite question: where are you from?" by Patricia Park on www.theguardian.com, 26 April 2013. |
| 80-81 | "African in America or African American?" by Mũkoma wa Ngũgĩ on www.theguardian.com, 14 January 2011. |
| 84-85 | "Warum die Amerikaner ihre Waffen so lieben" by Eric T. Hansen on www.zeit.de, 24 July 2012. |